BIBLE STUDY COMMENTARY

Kings and Chronicles

Bible Study Commentary

1 Kings—
2 Chronicles
ALAN MILLARD

Scripture Union
130, City Road, London EC1V 2NJ

CHRISTIAN LITERATURE CRUSADE
Fort Washington, Pennsylvania 19034

© 1985 Scripture Union
130 City Road, London EC1V 2NJ

First published 1985

ISBN 0 86201 299 6 (UK)
0 87508 155 x (USA)

Phototypeset in Great Britain by
Wyvern Typesetting Limited
Central Trading Estate, 277 Bath Road, Bristol BS4 3EH

Printed in Great Britain by
Ebenezer Baylis & Son Limited
The Trinity Press, Worcester, and London.

Cover photo: Jerusalem has always had to be fortified against her enemies. The present walls and towers were built in the sixteenth century AD.

General Introduction

The world-wide church in the last quarter of the twentieth century faces a number of challenges. In some places the church is growing rapidly and the pressing need is for an adequately trained leadership. Some Christians face persecution and need support and encouragement while others struggle with the inroads of apathy and secularism. We must come to terms, too, with the challenges presented by Marxism, Humanism, a belief that 'science' can conquer all the ills of mankind, and a whole range of Eastern religions and modern sects. If we are to make anything of this confused and confusing world it demands a faith which is solidly biblical.

Individual Christians, too, in their personal lives face a whole range of different needs – emotional, physical, psychological, mental. As we think more and more about our relationships with one another in the body of Christ and as we explore our various ministries in that body, as we discover new dimensions in worship and as we work at what it means to embody Christ in a fallen world, we need a solid base. And that base can only come through a relationship with Jesus Christ which is firmly founded on biblical truth.

The Bible, however, is not a magical book. It is not enough to say, 'I believe', and quote a few texts selected at random. We must be prepared to work with the text until our whole outlook is moulded by it. We must be ready to question our existing position and ask the true meaning of the word for us in our situation. All this demands careful study not only of the text but also of its background and of our culture. Above all it demands prayerful and expectant looking to the Spirit of God to bring the word home creatively to our own hearts and lives.

This new series of books has been commissioned in response to the repeated requests for something new to follow on from Bible Characters and Doctrines. It is now over ten years since the first series of Bible Study Books was produced and it is hoped that the new series will reflect the changes of the last ten years and bring the Bible text to life for a new generation of readers. The series has three aims:

1. To encourage regular, systematic personal Bible reading. Each volume is divided into sections ideally suited to daily use, and will normally provide material for three months (the exceptions being Psalms, four months, and Mark and Ezra-Job, two months). Used in this way the books will cover the entire Bible in five years. The comments aim to give background information and enlarge on the meaning of the text, with special reference to the contemporary relevance. Detailed questions of application are, however, often left to the reader. The questions for further study are designed to aid in this respect.

2. To provide a resource manual for group study. These books do not provide a detailed plan for week by week study. Nor do they present a group leader with a complete set of ready-made questions or activity

ideas. They do, however, provide the basic biblical material and, in the questions for further discussion, they give starting points for group discussion.

3. To built into a complete Bible commentary. There is, of course, no shortage of commentaries. Here, however, we have a difference. Rather than look at the text verse by verse the writers examine larger blocks of text, preserving the natural flow of the original thought and observing natural breaks.

Writers have based their comments on the Revised Standard Version and some have also used the New International Version in some detail. The books can, however, be used with any version.

Introduction to Kings and Chronicles

Kings and *Chronicles* are hardly the books of the Old Testament the Christian reader will turn to first for his daily strength. Yet the reader who perseveres will find them stimulating and rewarding. Some of the history they relate is well-known, but other episodes are obscure and sometimes difficult to understand. All are concerned with the history of God's people in the promised land. Established by the covenant of his grace offered to them at Sinai, they occupied Canaan to live there according to his laws to display his holiness and his standards for human life to the world. Their successes and failures, the conquests of their kings, and their defeats, their times of faithfulness to God and their spells of backsliding and apostasy can all be seen as illustrations of the varieties of human spiritual experience. In these inspired writings we learn how God dealt with his unruly nation, ultimately inflicting on them the punishments predicted in the Sinai revelation. Both books end, however, on a note of hope; God did not completely abandon Israel, he still had a mission for her.

In New Testament terms Israel's history was the preparation for the coming of the messiah. He could only fulfil his mission amongst a people who knew both God's love and grace, and his justice and mercy; a people who had been brought to realise the frailty and inconstancy, inadequacy and dependance of mortal man. Christ's coming marked the end of Israel as God's special nation, now his church would transcend all human limits. That did not by any means relegate Israel's history to the back shelf. The new Israel can learn constantly – and needs to do so – from the examples and lessons of the old and from the ways God worked with her. She, too, is founded on a covenant; she, too, is required to follow the laws of God as re-stated in the New Testament; she, too, is to display God's holy love and his standards to the world. While the national aspect is past, the church, locally and more widely, is a society with many comparable facets. *Kings* and *Chronicles* are rich in spiritual and practical teaching for individuals and for congregations.

For further information about places and characters mentioned in the text, and for maps, see the entries in *The Illustrated Bible Dictionary* (IVP, Leicester; Tyndale House Publishers, Wheaton, Illinois, 1980) or the identical text in *The New Bible Dictionary* (2nd ed., same publishers, 1982). These are mentioned occasionally in these Notes as *IBD* and *NBD*.

There is no up-to-date detailed commentary on *Kings*. For those who seek technical information, the volume by J. A. Montgomery and H. S. Gehman in the *International Critical Commentary* series (T. & T. Clark, Edinburgh, 1951) remains the most satisfactory. For *Chronicles*, H. G. M. Williamson's volume in the *New Century Bible* series (Marshall, Morgan, and Scott, London; W. B. Eerdmans, Grand Rapids, Michigan, 1982) offers a sober guide. The history of Israel during the monarchy is well-covered by D. F. Payne's *The Kingdoms of the Lord* (Paternoster Press, Exeter, 1982).

The Kingdoms of Israel and Judah: a chronological chart

– based on K. A. Kitchen and T. C. Mitchell, *Chronology of the Old Testament* in *IBD* 1 p. 273 (cf. *NBD*[2] pp. 196–7).

BC	JUDAH	(prophets)	ISRAEL
1060			
1040		Saul c. 1050–1010	
1020			
1000		David 1010–970	
980			
960		Solomon 970–930	
940	**JUDAH**		**ISRAEL**
920			
900	Rehoboam: 930–913 / Abijam:913–910 / Asa:910–869		Jeroboam I: 930–909 / Nadab: 909–908 / Baasha: 908–885
880			Zimri, Tibni:885–884 / Omri:884–873
860	Jehoshaphat: 869–848		Ahab: 873–853
840	Jehoram: 848–841 / Ahaziah: 841		Ahaziah: 853–852 / Joram: 852–841
820	Athaliah: 841–835 / Joash:835–796	ELIJAH / ELISHA	Jehu: 841–813
800			Jehoahaz: 813–798
780	Amaziah: 796–767		Jehoash: 798–781 / Jeroboam II: 781–753
760	Azariah: 767–739 (Uzziah)		
740		JONAH / AMOS	Zechariah: 753–752 / Shallum: 752
720	Jotham: 739–731 / Ahaz: 731–715 / Hezekiah: 715–686	HOSEA / MICAH	Menahem: 752–741 / Pekahiah: 741–739 / Pekah: 739–731
700		ISAIAH	Hoshea: 731–722
680	Manasseh: 686–641	ZEPHANIAH	
660			
640	Amon: 641–639 / Josiah: 639–609	NAHUM	
620		JEREMIAH	
600	Jehoahaz: 609 / Jehoiakim: 609–597		
580	Jehoiachin: 597 / Zedekiah: 597–587	EZEKIEL	

Rulers of Egypt, Syria, Assyria and Babylon, mentioned in Kings and Chronicles

	EGYPT	SYRIA	ASSYRIA & BABYLON
BC 940	Shishak 945–924		
920			
900			
880			
860		Ben-Hadad 860–843	Shalmaneser III 859–824
840		Hazael 843–796	
820			
800			
780			
760			
740			Tiglath-pileser III 745–727
720			Shalmaneser V 727–722
700			Sargon II: 722–705 Sennacherib: 705–681
680			Esarhaddon: 681–669
660			Ashurbanipal: 669–627
640			
620			**BABYLON**
600	Necho II 610–595		Nebuchadrezzar II 605–562
580			

Kings: Introduction

The books of Kings were designed to continue the narrative of 1 and 2 Samuel down to the end of the kingdom of Judah in 586BC. That means they cover about four hundred years, and were only completed at the end of that time. They were compiled from various writings and these are named occasionally. It is likely that a running account of events was kept at the court in Jerusalem, which supplied the basis. The bulk of Kings is written in a style and tone reminiscent of Deuteronomy. Judgements on the kings and the people, and the speeches in chapters 2 and 8 of 1 Kings, are notable examples. This style is often dated to the time of Jeremiah for his book is similarly written, but there is no reason why it should not be much older, a tradition going back to the time of Moses. Other ancient texts make it clear that features of style and tone like these could continue in use over many centuries.

The compilers of Kings, perhaps a line culminating in the final editor during the exile, intended to tell of the fortunes of their nation for the benefit of their own and future generations. They had to select from much more extensive accounts and, of course, they had a bias. Their bias, however, was not to paint Israel and Judah in the best light, it was to assess them in the light of God's laws, his written word, his continual instruction through the prophets and his acts in their history. One feature that sets these books apart from other ancient writings, and from many modern ones, is their frank admission of grave faults even in the greatest of the men portrayed and in the nation's life.

God's people, Israel, constituted a small nation and, in due course, two smaller kingdoms, among the rival states of the ancient Near East. Her history is heavily involved with her attempts to survive as an independent entity. The books of Kings show how she could, so long as she was faithful to God. Success was not an automatic result of obedience – some hardships are viewed as tests of faith – but it was seen as evidence of God's favour. At no time was Israel a victim of circumstances; the writers of Kings were convinced he controlled events, that he had brought Israel into existence and governed her every experience. He also controlled other nations, employing them to help or to chasten his people.

Israel's kings were especially important, for their attitudes as leaders played a major role in determining the people's conduct; but each member of the nation had his duty to God's laws and this, too, is made plain. The decisions of rulers could lead to many deaths, either through war, or, as these books show, through neglect of God's ways. Sorrow and destitution, riches and joy were all part of life in ancient Israel, as they are in modern societies. In the books of Kings they are seen as clearly as in other Old Testament books, and some ways of responding to such circumstances can also be seen.

1 and 2 Kings: Contents

1 Kings

1 David secures the succession

God's promises in the Old Testament usually involved future generations. As a promise-bearing leader grew old, therefore, the question of his successor became prominent. Hence the attention given to the deaths of Moses, Joshua and David. The moment of change opens the door to opportunists, and David had bred several through his numerous wives. Abishag, the girl who nursed the seventy-year old king, is introduced here (1–4) because of the later account of Adonijah's demand for her (2:17). Adonijah was David's fourth son (2 Sam. 3:4) and one who had been allowed his own way. Such people forget the lessons of the past (compare Absalom, 2 Sam. 15:1) and the claims of others; hence Adonijah's insistent, self-important claim, *I will be king*.

Adonijah's character won the allegiance of the soldier Joab and the priest Abiathar, two of David's long-established supporters. Was it for their own security they threw in their lot with him? The king was aged, but not yet dead, nor was his promise forgotten: Bathsheba had able supporters and Nathan was the man through whom God had given the oracle promising that David's line would continue to rule through Solomon (2 Sam. 7). Notice that David avoided violence; the royal authority, bodyguard and the proper form of institution (38,39) showed the real king. The anointing was a solemn ritual act to symbolise God's choice and the consecration of the king as his people's representative. His office was a holy and awesome one, as every position of responsibility for the well-being of others should be. Adonijah had offered only a banquet to build up his circle (again like Absalom, 2 Sam. 15:11). In treating his half-brother leniently, for undoubtedly Adonijah would have killed him (12), Solomon showed the potential for his future wisdom and inspired in others a willingness to trust him for the future.

David was aware that not only the throne was at stake: he intended that God's promise of the throne should be passed on to Solomon (17). His oath (29,30) had force behind it, for his many experiences of redemption gave convincing evidence that *the Lord lives*.

Notes: The mule (33) was preferred to the horse because it was more sure-footed in the hilly country. *En-Rogel* and *Gihon* (9,33) were springs outside Jerusalem, in the Hinnom valley to the south-west and the Kidron immediately to the east. As such they were public meeting places.

THOUGHT: Human ambition and self-interest can easily lead a person to anticipate God's plans, and may well cause others to take wrong steps.

2 Solomon's kingdom established

David's dying charge echoes Joshua's (Josh. 23;24), stressing God's promise of a continuing rule. There were two sides to the promise; failure by David's descendants could nullify its political side, yet it would continue in force until David's greater Son took up his kingdom. Observing the Deuteronomic law in every respect was the key to success, and that was not mere legalism, for the law asked for love. After the spiritual advice to ensure divine blessing came the political advice to ensure the stability of the throne, so far as human skill could do so. Joab had proved irresponsible earlier in taking revenge on other treacherous commanders in a way which reflected badly on king David; now he had taken Adonijah's part. Shimei had cursed David in God's name and David had let him live, forgiving the personal insult; but now this potential enemy saw his words proved wrong as Solomon ascended the throne (2 Sam. 16:5–13). His misuse of God's name deserved punishment, and Solomon could do what his father had sworn not to do (2 Sam. 19:16–23). Those who had aided David were commended to his son's kindness, for good deeds should not be forgotten more quickly than bad.

Adonijah had not lost his ambition. He sought to strengthen his position by taking his father's bed-fellow, though David had no relations with her (1:4), as Absalom had done (2 Sam. 16:21f). He won Bathsheba's favour, even though he misrepresented his position, ignoring the promises by which God overruled the natural succession man might expect (as with Jacob and Esau, Ephraim and Manasseh). But Adonijah could not hoodwink Bathsheba's son, who saw he could not trust him. Adonijah's fate was sealed and so was that of his supporters; Solomon's right to the throne and his family's place on it was assured, no threat from another line could continue (24). Further, Adonijah was asserting that God's oracles and promises were untrue. Even the sanctuary could not save Joab for he was proved guilty of deliberate killings (Exod. 21:14; Num. 35:33). Shimei tasted Solomon's grace, as Adonijah had done, yet failed to realise its deliberate temper. He went purposefully after his runaway slaves, disregarding his oath and so revealing that his values had not changed. With his death, David's story ends. The narrator collected these episodes together for tidiness, with no suggestion that they all happened before the events of the next chapters (39).

Notes: *slept with his fathers* (10) points to the family's solidarity through time.

THOUGHT: Can sudden pressing circumstances, like Shimei's, lead me to forget the obligations of the freedom God's grace has given me?

3 The best choice

In human terms, Solomon's marriage was a notable success for the beginning of a new reign. In her heyday, Egypt's pharaohs never gave their daughters to foreign kings, but at this date it was allowable. Other references to the princess in 1 Kings indicate the prestige of the marriage.

In spiritual terms Solomon's request marked his reign for success. Already in an attitude of worship, he was receptive to God's voice. The prestige attached to wisdom is evident in 4:29–34; 10:1–10. Solomon sought a greater measure and a higher quality than others possessed so that he could do his royal duty well to benefit his people, not for his own glory alone.

At Gibeon and at Jerusalem Solomon made burnt offerings, adding peace offerings in the capital which would cement the bond betwen the deity and the worshipper (Lev. 7:15–17). Then he entertained his court, establishing a similar bond with his people. Thus God, king and subjects were in harmony; only thus could God's people function properly as a nation. Throughout scripture, the act of eating together serves to satisfy more than physical need. The fellowship and friendship created at meals reach their climax in the meal which links God, Saviour and saved in harmony.

The story of the two harlots illustrates the king's exercise of his God-given gift. The vivid story gives a glimpse of low-level life, reminding us that Israelite society embraced as wide a variety as any. Knowing neither woman could be reckoned trustworthy, the king brought the truth to light by his violent proposal, and so revealed the character of each one (26). Israel was awed by Solomon's judgement and this case has become proverbial. It is impossible to tell how anyone else would have handled it since the story is so well known. What is vital to see is that 'the wisdom of God' is essential for every administrator in every situation, hence the call to pray for those in authority.

Notes: *Gibeon*, a few miles north of Jerusalem, was where the tabernacle had been erected (2 Chron. 1:3). *Go out or come in* (7), is a phrase for moving freely, doing business independently, as a free citizen.

THOUGHT: When the requests of God's people please him, they may receive much more. 'A wise and discerning mind' and understanding to 'discern between good and evil', are as essential to every individual serving God today as they were to Solomon.

4 Administrative practicalities

Every society requires organisation. Under Saul and David, Israel and Judah retained their tribal basis, with David giving his friends control (2 Sam. 8:15–18). Military conquest and the consolidation of Israel's hold on the land under David gave the opportunity to Solomon to construct regular systems of taxation and government. To head it Solomon had eleven men to David's six. They were his 'ministers'. As Paul advised the Roman Christians (Rom. 13:1–7), people have a responsibility to maintain their rulers for, however they rise to power, ultimately they owe their positions to God, a message the book of Kings conveys clearly. Solomon made twelve divisions in the land, in part only along the tribal boundaries, to provision his court. Verses 22, 23, 26, 27 give the basic amounts required (see note); we may suppose there were variations from time to time. The security David had given his realm brought a period of agricultural prosperity and freedom from raiders that permitted the regular tax to be paid without beggaring the land. The danger that it would become too heavy always lay just below the surface; and the royal tax, light or heavy, was a burden that the people had brought on themselves (1 Sam. 8). In the days of Solomon all was very well; verses 20,25 give traditional pictures of ideal life (compare the Rabshakeh's promise, 2 Kings 18:31) and are the fulfilment of God's promise to Abraham (Gen. 13:16; 22:17).

Solomon is portrayed as wise and knowledgeable. Scribes in Egyptian and Babylonian schools learnt lists of objects by category, and copied out proverbs and wise sayings as part of their language and writing exercises. Consequently, they were widely known. Solomon outshone all those famous in his day because his talents were God-inspired. The wisdom he accumulated through his own experiences and which he drew from others and approved, he crystallised in the book of Proverbs. There he shows how he saw lessons in all aspects of life, even in the most mundane, for everything is affected by man's attitude to his Creator.

Notes: The end of v. 19 is unclear; RSV emends the Hebrew slightly, contrast RV, NIV. For the extent of Solomon's empire (21,24) see *IBD* 3.1470 or a Bible Atlas. *Tiphsah* lay on the Euphrates. *40,000 stalls* (26): 2 Chronicles 9:25 had 4,000 which is in better proportion to the 1,400 chariots, so a scribal error may be assumed, see *Introduction* to Chronicles. On the *provisions* system in its ancient context, see K. A. Kitchen, *IBD, Food*.

THOUGHT: Proverbs 1:7 was the key to Solomon's success; make it your own.

5 Solomon's temple: basic materials

Israel was never isolated. David had subjugated or won the friendship of his neighbours and one, at least, wanted to sustain that friendship with David's son. Tyre and Sidon had been allotted to the tribe of Asher at the time of the conquest (Josh. 19:28,29) but had not been taken (Judg. 1:31,32) so now their resources had to be bought. Solomon proposed a purchase of a normal type, his own men working with Hiram's. The Tyrian king, who lived by trade, replied with a bargain to his own advantage. He had timber, but meagre food supplies; Israel had the reverse. The conclusion was satisfactory. *The Lord gave Solomon wisdom* (12) is repeated (3:12,28; 4:29) to stress that it applied in every sphere, from individual quarrels to international diplomacy. The treaty would have specified details of the timber sale, regulated other matters vital to good relations, and probably included a mutual aid agreement should either party be attacked. Solomon had no compunction about making a treaty with a pagan neighbour in order to gain the resources he needed for his work for God (7 is probably a polite acknowledgement that the Lord was acting for his people, rather than a statement of Hiram's faith). Does Luke 16:9 give a New Testament counterpart to Solomon's action?

Solomon's plans were labour-intensive; two months' work at home and one abroad for Israelite workers ensured minimal disruption of other activities. The 150,000 workers in the land were Canaanites and others who could hardly be trusted if they were sent abroad. As part of the Israelite kingdom, they were forced to join in the work in honour of Israel's God, whether they were willing or not. While their presence may have been an advantage to Israel at this moment, it was usually harmful, as the narratives of Judges show, and should not have continued after the conquest.

With timber available to span large halls, it was practical to use large squared stones for the walls. Otherwise rooms had to be quite narrow because local timber beams were not long. The Israelites had to learn from Phoenician craftsmen, descended from the Canaanites, for they had no experience of such elaborate construction work. Excavations show the high quality that was attained in buildings outside Jerusalem, especially at Megiddo.

Note: The Phoenician timber craftsmen were Sidonians (6), and the stone workers were Tyrians and Gebalites, that is men of Byblos (18).

THOUGHT: From the start Solomon wanted the best for the temple of his God, whatever the cost. What do I reckon the church deserves of my time and money?

6 Solomon's temple: the structure

This description gives an impression of a magnificent building which the writer had seen. It is not an architect's survey, some parts of it are difficult to interpret, so every modern reconstruction involves guesses. The central part, the temple proper, did not need to be large – 105 ft (32 m) long, 30 ft (9.2 m) wide, 52 ft (15 m) high – as only priests entered it. Lay worshippers stood in the courtyard beside the altar to see the sacrifices offered (see ch. 8). The sanctuary wall was built in diminishing stages so that beams could rest on the ledges to roof storage chambers beside it without need for socket holes penetrating the sanctuary wall.

Expensive masonry and elaborately carved cedar panelling were not enough for Solomon to honour his God; the whole interior had a gold overlay (the tabernacle gave a precedent). Fantastic as this may seem, Egyptian, Babylonian, and Assyrian kings displayed their wealth and power, and their respect for their gods, by plating temples with gold. Solomon followed the fashion of a great king. While intended for the only God, Solomon's temple resembled others in many ways. This was inevitable, for if it were totally different it would have been meaningless to non-Israelites, however sympathetic to Israel's faith. The temple had to be understandable to everybody. Closer inspection would reveal that it did differ in some important ways, principally in the absence of any statue of the god. This aspect of the temple has a parallel in the need for Christians to live and speak in a way that is intelligible to others in the world.

Notes: The cubical *inner sanctuary* – the holiest place, which only the high priest entered, on the atonement day – was entirely without light. *Cherubim* were imaginary creatures representing supernatural powers at God's command, guarding the ark. The doorways were probably one fifth (31) and one fourth (33) of the building's width, the larger doors having folding sections, rather than having shaped lintels as RSV indicates. The archaic names of the months *Ziv* and *Bul* (1,38) had to be explained for readers of later times. *Four hundred and eightieth year:* with Solomon's accession c.970 BC, the temple began c.966 BC., a simple addition setting the exodus at c.1446 BC. While some scholars accept this reckoning, many explain it as a comprehensive total of all the judges, together with Moses, Joshua, Saul, and David, not as an exact interval (see *IBD*, *Chronology*).

THOUGHT: There was a condition in God's presence with Israel (12,13): there is a condition in God's presence with the Christian (John 14:15–17).

7 Solomon's palace and temple equipment

The author turns from the temple to the king's palaces. These took longer to build, for they were larger and more varied, to hold the necessary officials and staff for the court of a great king. The House of the Forest of Lebanon was a great pillared hall – 150 ft (46 m) long, 75 ft (23 m) wide, 45 ft (13.8 m) high – with flanking chambers. The form is known from Egyptian and other examples. It probably served as an office for the administration and as a treasury. The Hall of Pillars served some other purpose. Appropriately, the Judgement or Throne Hall adjoined the king's quarters. The queen had comparable accommodation; and all these buildings were beside the temple, to the north of the original city of Jerusalem.

From the structures, the author turns to the furnishings of the temple. His account reads as if it were copied from a record of the work done, or an inventory; certainly ancient clerks kept such documents with details like these. No-one has explained the bronze pillars convincingly, although archaeological discoveries suggest they were features of Canaanite shrines. *Jachin* means 'he will establish', and *Boaz*, 'in him is strength', which some suppose were key words of oracles about the dynasty of David. The sea (23–26) was a gigantic basin to supply water for washing, essential when numbers of animals were slaughtered in sacrifice daily. Its capacity is reckoned at 10,000 to 20,000 gallons. Again, huge basins are attested from ancient times, though none that survive are so large. The bronze stands were of a kind known from models found in Canaan and Cyprus (*IBD*. 1528). They were small trolleys for moving washing bowls (lavers). All the rites of Israel's worship had to have appropriate instruments and vessels and Solomon ensured that all were of the best possible quality. God could not be worshipped fully by his people, the chosen nation, without their observing every prescribed action which laid stress on the opposition of holiness to sin and the difficulty of bridging the gap between God and man. The major national festivals were not man's inventions with gaudy paraphernalia to bring superficial feelings of goodwill, but God's commands which were designed to bring deep peace and joy to those who observed them properly.

Notes: *cedar beams* (11,12) apparently formed a framework in the stone courses to prevent collapse through earthquake shocks. Gold *sockets* for doors (50): ancient Assyrian texts also mention door fittings of gold.

THOUGHT: When a wealthy king wanted to show his devotion to God, he brought the best he could. So did other wise men (Matt. 2:11) and early Christians (e.g. 2 Cor. 8:1–5). The example is to be copied (2 Cor. 9:6–15).

Questions for further study and discussion on 1 Kings 1–7

1. Solomon's accession was disrupted by his half-brother, a common enough case of a father's behaviour affecting his descendants. Read 2 Samuel 11,12 and consider why it was Solomon who followed David.

2. Were Solomon's actions to secure his throne entirely self-interested? How far can they be justified in the light of the king's role as judge (7:7) and God's appointed deputy?

3. Can lavish expenditure on a religious building such as Solomon's temple have any place in Christianity today?

4. Notice the details of the temple and its equipment; each one contributed to the glory of the whole. How does this compare with the structure of the church (1 Cor. 12:12–28)?

5. In what ways may Christians use the talents of non-Christians to aid worship and service? Are there any limits?

6. Does the burden of taxation that Israel had to carry to support her kings and their state find any parallel in the demands a large central organisation or hierarchy may place on churches today? If Israel's monarchy was no part of God's plan for his people at the start, is there a place for big organisations to govern our local churches today?

8:1–21 Solomon's temple: the opening

The temple was to be God's earthly house, the centre of the nation's worship; not a private chapel, nor one temple among many. Into its innermost sanctuary the priests carried the ark containing the tablets of the law. These bore the covenant between God and Israel, the basis of the nation's existence (9). On that the temple was erected, and through it Solomon could approach God in the praise and prayer that follow. Although the ark itself was hidden from all except the high priest, the carrying poles projecting into the holy place assured the priests daily that the ark was still there and that the covenant which it guarded was therefore still in force. That meant God was ready to receive all who came, on his terms, to him. As he had when the tabernacle was dedicated (Exod. 40), so now God made his presence visible.

Solomon's words are retrospective (12–21) and prospective (22–66). First, his expression of wonder that God should deign to dwell with man (27), for his nature is so different and unknowable except by his grace (Deut. 4:11). The RSV follows the Greek version in contrasting the brightness of God's created sun with his own impenetrable divinity. Solomon expresses an awe of God's Person which has tended to diminish since the new revelation brought by the incarnation, though it should not have done. In 15–21 he recalls God's faithfulness and his parallel grace, past and continuing. Through them came the choice of God's people, their preservation, the choice of David as God's ruler and then Jerusalem as the place for the temple. Thus Solomon's work was the capstone, completing the plan envisaged at Sinai. All should now be in order for Israel to flourish and display the goodness of God (59,60). The only threat to this comes from the people themselves (22–51).

The temple was the central shrine of Israel. The ruling of Deuteronomy ch. 12 is not hard to understand and Solomon's building could not be rivalled. Yet the urge to worship at local shrines never ceased; man's will has always been to do as he sees fit (see Deut. 12:8), 'one Church, one Faith, one Lord' is more theory than practice. The physical temple was a vital symbol to Israel of God's presence, yet was easily taken as a talisman and abused as a guarantee, however Israel behaved.

THOUGHT: What is the difference between our private worship of God and our worship of him with others in a church building? Why do we need both aspects?

8:22–66 Solomon's Temple: dedication

God's past treatment of Israel was the ground for hope (26). Solomon was aware that no temple could contain God, yet God had promised his presence and now had shown it. Nevertheless, the king's prayer was addressed to God in heaven, although it was directed through the temple (29,30) because of the ark.

Solomon lists occasions needing God's forgiveness, fully aware that his people would turn to God mostly after sinning. Repeatedly, he refers to sins they might commit (33,35,38–39,46–47), sins arising from the human heart and from which none are free (38,46). He was equally aware of God's merciful nature. As God's chosen ruler, Solomon was in a special position to intercede for the nation. Only the first occasion of sin mentioned concerns the individual Israelite and probably refers to the sort of case which no human power could resolve: the perjurer could expect God to punish him. Solomon clearly assumes that should the nation find itself in trouble it would be because of sin – a common view, but not the only answer (John 9:2,3). He names typical, and probably the most common troubles (31–40). Verses 41–43 give an important statement of Israel's role as an example to the world (compare 59,60). The king expected aliens to come to the temple, as God's people should always expect unbelievers to be attracted to the place where he is (1 Cor. 14:22–25). Solomon also expected trouble leading to war, and sought God's aid for the needy people. This would be a defensive war, we may assume, rather than an Israelite act of aggression (eg. 2 Sam. 10; 2 Chron. 14:9–15). Verses 46–51 cover the ultimate tragedy, loss of the Promised Land, which might seem to mark the end of Israel and the failure of the covenant. In the light of Deuteronomy 30, Solomon believed God would not totally disown his people. He readily envisaged Israelites praying to God in distant lands and being heard; God was not localised. Israel's royal shepherd prayed not only for Israel's sake, but also for God's glory. That is reflected in the way God's people behave and the events that befall them (51,53,60).

The enormous sacrifices (63,64) would feed the assembled people, being peace offerings (see Lev. 7:11–18). Compare the figures with the court's daily supply (4:23). Solomon shared his wealth with his people as well as with his God in the temple.

THOUGHT: Translate Solomon's prayer into Christian terms, with the church as Israel, and then with yourself in that position.

9 A conditional glory

His great buildings complete, Solomon might be pardoned a little pride, but he was reminded that he should be as faithful as he had called his people to be if his line and temple were to last. God promised his presence for ever (3), for he had declared the temple worthy (8:10). However much Solomon might devote to the temple, it was by God's grace alone that it could serve its purpose. The promise was not unconditional; there was an essential, yet easily ignored, 'if', as in so many divine promises. The condition applied to the royal line, the promised land, and the temple. None were safe from the effects of human failure and Solomon needed to be reminded of that at the moment of his greatest prosperity. Here is the response to Solomon's prayer in ch. 8, equally cognisant of these possibilities, unthinkable though they might appear at such a time. It is a warning, not a threat. The temple's fate would be the reverse of 8:41–43, negating its purpose. It may appear extreme, yet it would be essential for maintaining the reputation of the One whose name had been set there. The remainder of 1 and 2 Kings exhibits God's grace in allowing his people to enjoy their land, royal line and temple for so long in a state very far from the jubilant loyalty of this moment.

The varied details of Solomon's rule (15–28) demonstrate the king's prosperity in every sphere. Even the dissatisfaction of his Tyrian ally was overcome. The cities in the area were given a name which means 'defective, crippled'.

Solomon ensured his own cities were well fortified and garrisoned. City gates uncovered by archaeologists at Hazor, Megiddo, and Gezer (15) show almost identical plans and can be dated to Solomon's time, attesting a strong ruler's central control and resources. Gezer (16) had never been securely Israelite, although on the main route from the coast to Jerusalem. The Millo (15,24) may have been an artificial terrace in Jerusalem. Conquered Canaanites laboured on these construction works, supervised by 550 Israelite officers (23), unlike the temple and palace building which needed Israelite labour as well (5:13ff).

The collocation of verses 24 and 25 is ominous, as later chapters will show.

The statement that Solomon offered sacrifices and burnt incense (25) should be understood as meaning he commanded these acts, not that he did them himself, which would be contrary to the ritual laws.

THOUGHT: To what extent are God's promises still conditional?

10 An attractive glory

Solomon's tremendous success was known far and wide and was coupled with the 'name of the Lord'. Material prosperity was a clear sign of divine approval to ancient man for they did not compartmentalise the aspects of life, realising that it is an integrated whole. So the Queen of Sheba did not travel just to admire Solomon's display but to find out if he deserved his glory. She went home convinced and with praise to the Lord. Solomon's witness was good, his visitor gave credit where it was due (9, compare Matt. 5:16). She also gave great gifts to demonstrate her conviction, and received others from her host. Other people followed her example. Here the prosperity of God's king served to secure good relations with others who were not believers, as well as advertising the grace and goodness of God.

The enormous quantities of gold (the queen of Sheba brought about four tons) entered the royal treasury. These huge amounts become more credible than many have supposed when viewed beside other figures from the ancient world which there is no reason to doubt. Some of the gold paid for and decorated the royal palace, the throne and the king's table (14–22). It was important that the great king should be seen to have all the normal trappings of power. How much of this wealth reached ordinary Israelites we cannot know; the writer implies that citizens of the capital, at least, had some share (27) and the trading ventures would have involved others. Solomon's wealth, nonetheless, provokes thought. Was God's promise of riches simply to make the king great in human terms? Is the possession of a great fortune justifiable in a world full of deprivation? What good came from Solomon's wealth? When the quantities of gold were notable, silver was common (27). Soon silver would be prized because the gold had gone, and bronze shields replace those of gold (14:27). Man's estimation of gold is quite irrational, and the ultimate worthlessness to Israel of Solomon's store (taken away to Egypt, 14:25,26) teaches that lasting treasure is of a different sort (Matt. 6:19–21).

Notes: *Sheba* (1) lay in southern Arabia, the area of modern Yemen. Gold shields (16,17) adorned temples in other states, according to ancient records. *Kue* (28) was in Cilicia, south-central Turkey, near the Mediterranean coast.

THOUGHT: Here is the fulfilment of the promise of 3:13; have you seen God give you more than you expected? How have you handled this and with what effects?

11:1–25 Solomon's shame

The possible pitfalls of prosperity had been plain to Solomon as his reign began and when he dedicated the temple (2:1–4; ch. 8). Like Adam and Eve, he had everything in his favour, yet he fell. At what point the decline began is not clear. David had been polygamous, so Solomon's harem probably grew from his accession. However, this was not as heinous as the polytheism it led him to in his later years (4). He had no excuse (9,10) and could have anticipated his condemnation (11; see v. 2; 9:3–9). His actions were public (7), doubtless noted by his subjects and duly imitated. What he had feared his people might do, he led them into doing himself. His prestige and wealth brought the numerous women to him, but his wisdom failed to show that his personal behaviour needed to display the highest integrity.

Solomon's sin brought a message from God (whether by a prophet or a dream is not related, the fact of it is not doubted). Punishment was as certain for his fault as for his father's (2 Sam. 12), but whereas David's sin was against a man and God's law, Solomon's was against God, striking at the root of Israel's *raison d'etre* (8:59,60). Repentance is given no place here, but still God's judgement is tempered: Solomon himself would keep his kingdom and would rule for the rest of his days, though knowing that his son would lose all the glory he had acquired, that he had marred God's promise, and that his own continuance was only for the sake of his father, David. How much, and how unwittingly, a father may affect his son's life!

The empire began to disintegrate in Solomon's lifetime, so he saw the fruit of his weakness. It is not clear how early in the reign Hadad returned from his refuge in Egypt. His activities would have disrupted trade coming from the Red Sea and Arabia, and forced Israel into military action to protect her interests. The Pharaoh was probably the one who was Solomon's brother-in-law, engaging in a policy that would curtail Israel's power. Rezon was a more serious threat, eventually gaining control of Damascus, a jewel in David's empire, establishing its independence to make it a continuing foe of Israel.

Note: Verses 1 and 2 make it clear that Solomon's harem was developed for his own gratification, not purely to make good diplomatic relations with neighbouring kings.

THOUGHT: Solomon did evil and did not wholly follow the Lord. How wholly do I follow?

11:26–12:24 Israel's secession

Solomon's greatest threat came from within his realm. One of his promising young protégés received an oracle. Jeroboam, in charge of the labour force for the central part of the land (*house of Joseph* = Ephraim and Manasseh) may have had no seditious plans until he met God's prophet. Ahijah's vivid gesture made his message plain. The reason for the division was also made plain and a promise was offered like the promise made to David. The difference was that the Davidic line would continue (11:36) and eventually find relief (11:39), the lamp symbolising continuing life (see 2 Sam. 14:7). There could be two God-fearing kingdoms, if Jeroboam kept his word. When Solomon came to know of this prophecy, Jeroboam found refuge with Shishak, a new pharaoh of Egypt who had displaced the king whose daughter Solomon married. Shishak worked to defeat Israel.

Wise Solomon had a foolish son. Rehoboam wanted to enjoy the same luxury as his father without recognising that it had not been Solomon's by right but by God's grace. His friends' advice was simply sycophancy; the experienced elders had a long-term concern. They knew that care for the nation at the start of the reign would bring long-lasting loyalty. Whatever the origin of Solomon's glory and whatever benefits had flowed from it, the people had evidently borne a heavy load; they deserved a rest. Rehoboam expected to be crowned in the centre of the land – the heart of the tribes of Joseph and the seat of Jeroboam's support. There Joshua and Israel had celebrated God's covenant long before (Josh. 8:30–35). Now Israel was to repudiate the covenant with David, taking up an old cry (2 Sam. 20:1) and displaying their scorn for Rehoboam by lynching his officer. Rehoboam's final folly was frustrated by another prophet who spoke both to king and to people.

Israel and Judah were now two separate states. The biblical historian claims this was God's doing, a punishment for Solomon's idolatry (11:33). The subsequent history of Israel hardly suggests that this was a good thing, but it is possible to maintain that benefits could have come from such a division had the people continued in the right way. Perhaps most noteworthy is God's readiness to maintain a new king, Jeroboam, so long as he proved faithful. No one, not even David, could expect God's favour to be given irrespective of his conduct. At this point and for a long time afterwards, it was not the people whom God rejected, but their king.

THOUGHT: Does the origin of the division have any lessons for churches today?

On what grounds, if any, can the division of a local church be justified?

12:25–13 Jeroboam and the word of God

Dividing Judah from Israel brought several problems. The first was to find a suitable capital city for the northern kingdom. Shechem was central but not easy to defend, being under the shadow of Mount Ebal and Mount Gerizim. Penuel lay to the east of Jordan, too distant for proper control. The site was not fixed until Omri's day. Related to the capital was the question of a religious focus. Jeroboam naturally thought that to continue the link with Jerusalem would give his rival king a great advantage. His solution, creating new gods for his people, was worse than Solomon's sin. Even if they were meant to represent the Lord, the concept was contrary to his laws. The new shrines marked the limits of the new realm, almost as frontier guards. Their cult, priests, and sacrifices had the pattern of the Jerusalem worship, with a festival in the eighth month probably corresponding to the feast of tabernacles of the previous month (Lev. 23:33,34). The unnamed gold calves stood for strength and fertility, echoing the bad episode at Sinai (Exod. 32, especially 4). The Israelites did think they were emblems of the Lord, rather than of some other deity; and the fact that their personal names continued to be composed with the element *Yah-* or *-yah*, a shortened form of 'Yahweh', the divine name, is evidence of their belief (as seen in Ahaz*iah*, *Jeho*ash etc.). Everything was done, therefore, to make their religious practice appear no different from the true worship of God.

Jeroboam forfeited the promise of 11:37,38 at the moment of its fulfilment. An anonymous prophet from the other kingdom crossed the border to bring home the seriousness of his action. His prophecy is one of the few to name someone long before his birth, almost three hundred years in this case. Consequently, all who reject the inspiration of scripture assume that these words were inserted in Josiah's day, or later.

The prophet carried out his commission, yet failed to follow his instructions. Deceived by the old prophet of Bethel, he ate and drank in the apostate kingdom. His compromise was punished severely, though his corpse was spared the lion's savaging. Did the prophet of Bethel hope for God's blessing by entertaining one who came to do what he had not done, to condemn the king? The Judean prophet too readily accepted as God's word what contradicted his own understanding.

Note: *Samaria* (13:32) may be a modernisation of an older name, or indicate that the name was used before Omri built his city.

THOUGHT: How often, and against what, do we 'test all things' (see Gal. 1:6–9; Col. 2:8, 2 Tim. 2:11–19)?

Questions for further study and discussion on 1 Kings 8–13

1. Solomon's sin brought disaster to his family in the reduction of his realm, and to his nation in the loss of the empire. Damascus and Edom threatened Israel and Judah for the rest of their history. Apostasy ensnared all of Israel's kings and most of Judah's, becoming the historian's touchstone (14:22; 15:3 etc.). Is there any ground for supposing that a link still exists between a nation's spiritual stance and its material and political prosperity?

2. The temple was the focus of Israel's worship, both nationally and individually. How would you explain to an Israelite the absence of a central shrine for Christians?

3. Meditate upon Luke 12:27–31; how does Solomon's life measure against these words, bearing in mind his initial request of God; and how does yours?

4. Could a Christian lead his nation in a revolution as Jeroboam did, at a prophet's word; or is such action outside the Christian's calling?

14 Two reigns end

Jeroboam still hoped for God's help. Ahijah's presence within his kingdom should have kept him aware of the condition of God's promise, even if the prophet was too old to be very active. The prophet whose words had spurred Jeroboam to the throne now spoke his doom. The charge lies in verse 9. However awkward the situation (12:27), the king should not have broken God's law. Sick Ahijah would die naturally, not so his brothers (10,11; 15:27–29). The promise to Jeroboam had been a dynasty as promised to David (11:38). David's dynasty continued, impoverished, because of David's faith, despite the succession of disloyal kings. Jeroboam showed none of that faith, so his line perished quickly. Ahijah's words underline the role of God in exalting Jeroboam, in abasing him, and in replacing him (*I*, 7, 10; *he*, 14–16), and Jeroboam's responsibility in bringing God's punishment on Israel (*yet you . . . but you . . .* 8,9). The king's evil would affect the nation. In a vivid picture the nation's years of insecurity and eventual destruction are forecast (15). At the conquest the Euphrates was set as one boundary of the promised land (Josh. 1:4); the exile, which dispersed the national force beyond that boundary, would illustrate the forfeiture of God's favour (16). The Asherim, the golden calves and other idols which followed in their wake, were symptoms of the nation's weakness.

Consulting a prophet to learn the outcome of an illness was a regular practice (eg. 2 Kings 1:2). A disguise was adopted, perhaps in the hope of hearing a more precise response than a king might obtain, or because of fear there would be no answer for a king out of divine favour (compare 1 Sam. 28:15,16). The practice was entirely contrary to the laws of Israel.

Jeroboam's reign held no more of interest to the historian of Kings, he referred curious readers to a record apparently begun at this time (19).

In Judah, Rehoboam – half Ammonite, so perhaps attracted to the worship of Milcom (11:5) – allowed wholesale polytheism. The Canaanite cults were primarily aimed at ensuring fertility and so prosperity, appealing to the basic human appetites. Partly as a consequence, five years after Solomon's death the signs of his wealth were taken away and the temple was stripped of its material splendour. Shishak (11:40) has left, carved on a temple wall, a list of places his army conquered in Palestine. His son gave considerable treasure to the gods of Egypt, presumably including some of the spoil of Jerusalem and the gold Solomon had given to his God.

THOUGHT: Consider the differences and similarities between Rehoboam and Jeroboam. How and why did God's attitude to them differ?

15 Two lines of kings

The histories of the two kingdoms are related in parallel form from Rehoboam and Jeroboam onwards, with synchronisms between the kings. Rehoboam's son did nothing very praiseworthy, although he does not appear to have been so wicked as some later kings. His brief reign simply testified to God's continuing grace to David's house (4). Verses 6 and 7 emphasise the circumstances of continuing warfare in which he lived; 2 Chronicles 13 gives details.

Abijam's son Asa, who followed, was a completely different character. His long reign saw religious reform, reaching even to his grandmother's status, although the *high places* continued as centres of unorthodox worship. The male cult prostitutes and idols were legacies of the pagan cults of the Canaanites which Israel had failed to eradicate when she conquered the promised land. The old queen mother's *Asherah* showed how far the evil had spread. *Asherah* was the ever-popular mother and lover, common in all human societies, however disguised.

Hostilities with Israel continued, the northerners establishing a garrison to command the road north from Jerusalem to Ramah, only eight miles (twelve km.) from the city. Asa found himself too weak to fend off his foe, but by buying aid from a foreign king he involved strangers in Israel's affairs. The Syrian was entirely mercenary, without any loyalty to his existing ally. The plan worked, and eventually the Judeans built two forts with the materials from Baasha's. Israel was deprived of land and temporarily cowed.

Baasha had been the instrument for ending the line of Jeroboam which had completely failed to fulfil the conditions of God's promise (11:37,38). Killing the head of Jeroboam's family was not enough, the whole family had to be exterminated, for sin is contagious and the promise could not be allowed any possibility of further claims upon it; the line had forfeited any right to it (29,30). Further, Baasha may have feared revenge had any of Jeroboam's relatives lived. Thus began the pattern of assassinations that brought instability to Israel throughout her history. Baasha failed to learn from the events he was involved in. He looked only for his own advantage and eventually found himself ruler of a much smaller realm than his predecessor. The enmity between Israel and Philistia smouldered for the next twenty-five years (see 16:16). Gibbethon was in the north of Philistine territory, west of Gezer.

THOUGHT: Asa took back what he had given to God (15) in order to buy human help (18), treating the temple as a safe deposit. Do we give to God, or only lend?

16 Evil in Israel

Although Baasha brought God's punishment upon Jeroboam, he had to pay the penalty for his deed (7). His line lasted no longer than his victim's; like Jeroboam, he was warned of his fate but turned a deaf ear to the prophetic urgings, despite their colourful threats. Elah, his son, was as bad, as his conduct illustrates (9). The wheel of assassination turned, Zimri slaughtered Baasha's family. Then, once it was seen that kings were made so easily, civil war broke out. Zimri killed himself (there was no place for ex-kings) and the Omri faction beat all others.

Omri was an important leader, although he did nothing that really interested the Hebrew historian. He bought the site for his new capital as a private estate. Samaria is a strategic hill with long views, commanding routes in all directions. Other ancient records reveal that Omri conquered part of Moab and held it for Israel, and that it was his name which was used by foreigners for the region of Samaria (Beth Omri). Political success was less important to the biblical historian than Omri's black record of idolatry (25).

The verdict on Omri is surpassed by his son's. Ahab was not simply idolatrous, his conduct was deliberate provocation (33), as the next chapters show. Ahab was the epitome of an evil king. Jeroboam may have erected images for Israel's God, Ahab built a shrine for Baal in Samaria, where we never hear of a shrine for the Lord, and he erected an emblem of Asherah. The Baal temple may have begun as an attempt to make his wife feel at ease, as Solomon had tried to do for his foreign wives (11:7,8). Ahab's wife was to prove to be his evil genius. Instead of accepting the ways of his home, she worked hard to impose those of her own. Marriage to the neighbouring king's daughter was doubtless a wise political move, but Ahab had not weighed that advantage against other aspects nor felt it overrode them. Do we have here an example of a wicked man deliberately planning evil?

Jericho had lain under a curse since Joshua's day. As the first city to fall to Israel, it had been dedicated to God like the first-fruits of harvest. Rebuilding it was a sign of popular disobedience and it brought the curse into action. Notice how there continued to be faithful men who spoke for God in those dark days.

THOUGHT: Is there any justification for a Christian to marry a non-Christian? Can Ahab's example and Paul's words (2 Cor. 6:14,15) be disregarded in churches today?

17 Needs supplied

The wicked Ahab was introduced in ch. 16; to oppose him, God raised a man of no standing, Elijah, whose father's name is not given. His home, Tishbe, lay east of the Jordan, on the bank of the brook Cherith, but within Israel's borders. His name is significant in the light of the history of his life, 'My God is Yahweh'.

Elijah's first act was dramatic. No circumstances are portrayed, he simply told Ahab of the drought he was bringing in God's name. The prophet himself would suffer unless God supported him. In his remote refuge his suppliers were ravens, large scavenging birds that could carry pieces of food across the countryside. (Some commentators equate the Hebrew word for ravens with one for bedouin, and suggest local nomads fed the prophet, but this still leaves the problem of where they could have found the food. He who controlled the rain also controlled the birds.)

Yet Elijah's supply ended. He had to leave Israelite territory for the area of Sidon. The drought extended beyond Israel to Baal's homeland. In his need Elijah asked help from one least able to afford it, from a widow, one of the class most at risk in ancient times (see, for example, Deut. 10:18; 14:29). Moreover, this woman was down to her last handful of flour. Still the prophet persisted in asking for his share first. Had he some intimation that God would work a miracle? His personality in some way convinced her and her reward was immediate. Elijah appeared to be a friend but, when her son fell ill, the widow assumed, as many would, that she was being punished by God. She reproached God's spokesman (18) and Elijah also questioned God's purpose but from a different basis (20), for he believed in God. She, at that point, did not. As God honoured her response to Elijah, so he did Elijah's prayer of faith. Whether it was by 'the kiss of life' or by other means, the child's life was restored through God's will. Elijah's prayer makes it clear the child was dead. Elijah then had his reward in the mother's words: no longer did she speak of *your God* but of *God*, she had seen and now believed God's word to be true – and she was not an Israelite. Jesus built on this event in his rebuke of the Jewish leaders in Luke 4:26, in words that still need to be heeded today.

Note: *Zarephath*, modern Sarafand, lies 8 miles (12 km.) south of Sidon.

THOUGHT: Is Elijah's demand of the widow a reminder to give God his share first, whatever the circumstances? Is there a principal here of setting the needs of others before one's own at all times?

18 God versus Baal (1): reality versus illusion

Elijah's next command was to return home to face the hostile king. Ahab was to be shown that the drought was no coincidence: God controlled the rain. The king had pursued Elijah relentlessly using his good relations with other states without success; God kept his man for his moment. Unknown to Elijah (22), others were still faithful. Ahab's chamberlain, whose name means 'servant of the Lord', risked his master's anger to save some; how they were chosen to survive (13) is a hidden part of the divine purpose. Now Obadiah gibed at the request of the most-wanted man in Israel, fearful because of the prophet's very elusiveness (12). If his information proved useless, Ahab would execute him, yet surely his righteousness did not deserve that. Could he trust Elijah? Elijah's oath (15) accomplished what Ahab's could not (10).

Verse 17 reveals how perverted Ahab's view was. The whole story illustrates the conflict of God's reality with man's illusion. Baal was a human concept, and like man – self-centred, self-conscious, capricious, unreliable. The 'lord' (Baal) man had made in his own image was the reverse of the Lord who made man in his image. Baal demanded sacrifice, attention and services from his worshippers, who could then go and do as they pleased. With such a god society has no controls, no higher authority; each man is free to seek his own advantage, as the story of Naboth will show (ch. 21). Its appeal to the natural man is obvious. Utterly opposite is the religion of Israel with its strict moral code set down by the God who demanded complete obedience out of love and gratitude. His actions had shown that his word was reliable, that his nature did not change and that he cared for his people. Here was the distinction between Israel and her neighbours, between revealed religion and human concoction. Because it did not spring from man's mind, the basis of Israelite society was at least as much concern for your neighbour as for yourself. All this Israel had known and Ahab had rejected, spurred on by his heathen queen.

Is it a weakness of man that he needs a guide from outside? Without such a guide he is constantly pulled by opposing forces. Even in Eden Adam had to make a decision and his wrong choice was the first of a continuing series. Had Baal created man, or man made himself, we may wonder what liberty or choice he would have allowed him, and how much self-sufficiency.

THOUGHT: Compare Obadiah's faith and actions with Elijah's. How far can circumstances affect the witness of God's servants?

18 God versus Baal (2): reality wins

Elijah had to prove that Israel's God was active, and Baal impotent. The people, being undecided, were ready to follow the result of a fair test. Elijah's proposals were simple but left no room for fraud. He allowed his opponents every advantage so that their failure would point to the completeness of their illusion. Their self-mutilation, a means to compel the god to pay attention, was forbidden to the Israelites (eg. Lev. 19:28), whose God demanded physical wholeness in his priests (Lev. 21:16–24). Elijah's taunts ridicule the concept of Baal; how could a god be so localised! How could anyone worship a figure who could be reduced to such terms! Repeated phrases (26,29) underline the futility of the baalists.

On Mount Carmel men had worshipped God in the past. The rebuilt altar testified that it was the Lord who created Israel. Although only the northern kingdom was involved, that altar represented all twelve tribes, for the power of God shown to only one could affect all God's people.

Elijah was determined to prove the supremacy of his Lord. The water and the small trench to hold it displayed his faith and his contempt for Baal. At the time of the afternoon lamb sacrifice in Jerusalem (Exod. 29:38–39), Elijah called on God, seeking proof of God's reality for the audience and so of his own calling and conduct. In addition to controlling the elements, God is asked for proof that he controls his people (37, see Notes). The people had their answer, accepted it, and acted on it. Vindicated, Elijah executed Baal's prophets to rid the land of their poison. Ahab was humiliated and Jezebel's hatred heightened (19:2).

To re-assert God's control of all, Elijah forecast the longed-for rain (41, refer back to 17:1). The immediate contest being won, and the people convinced of the spiritual truth, he could concentrate on supplying their physical need. Was the delay (43,44) a test of faith for the prophet, king, and people? The message to Ahab was another show of strength: he'd better hurry or he'd be caught by God's rain, travelling the sixteen miles (26 km.) to Jezreel. Elijah even beat Ahab on that journey; he understood what Paul was later to tell Timothy (1 Tim. 4:8)!

Notes: *turned their hearts back* (37) may mean either to repentance, or to backslide in the first place. Verse 38: explaining the fire in terms of oil poured on the altar, or of lightning from the cloudless sky devalues the whole story.

THOUGHT: Elijah fought for God on terms the audience accepted, armed with his own faith for attack. How can we meet non-Christians on terms they can accept in order to present Christian realities?

19 Elijah faces reality

Jezebel was not cowed by the Carmel display. She would be rid of the 'troubler' who hindered her aim of bringing Israel under Baal's control. Fleeing south, Elijah gave up. His prayer is almost a reproach, called forth by despair at events and by misunderstanding God's ways, as had been his prayer at Zarephath (17:20). Had he thought God had chosen him because he was better than his fathers (4)? Elijah had to learn that God does not work as man expects, nor reveal the whole course of his plans, though he does not leave his men without any idea of his ways (Amos 3:7). Foodless and hopeless, almost in the position of the priests of Baal on Mount Carmel, the angel found him and gave him strength to travel, telling him, the reader assumes, his destination. Note that he had to go on without knowing what would happen.

Horeb was the mountain where, in thunder and lightning, smoke and fire, God had made the covenant that established Israel as his nation (Exod. chas. 19–31). Elijah affirmed that the covenant had been rejected and believed he alone remained faithful. What followed showed him that God's ways were not always the same. Where Moses stood before the awesome grandeur of God's majesty, Elijah met him in a 'still, small voice'. He learnt the lesson of Zechariah 4:6. Protesting his own loyalty again, he was told to inaugurate changes in Damascus and in Israel.

Reassurance of human fellowship (18) was supported by the designation of his successor; he would not be alone any more. Although Elijah did not, so far as the record tells, anoint Hazael and Jehu, he did it in effect through Elisha, his heir acting in his place. Throwing his mantle over Elisha was a way of showing that Elijah had taken him under his responsibility (compare Ruth 3:9ff). Elisha's action clearly ended his farming life. His new role was like Joshua's (Num. 27:18f; Josh. 1:1). Note that Elijah's reply to Elisha was probably, 'Yes, go back, what have I done to you (to prevent you)?'

Elijah's experience at Mount Horeb contrasted with Moses' in several ways, yet it was also parallel in others and was one of the points of likeness between the two which coupled them in the appearance at the transfiguration.

THOUGHT: 'the Lord was not in . .' (12); should we seek him in mighty acts and great revivals or in single conversions and individual devotion? Is this a proper contrast?

Questions for further study and discussion on 1 Kings 14–19

1. Can it be said that God was playing with Jeroboam as if he were a puppet in making a promise to him, giving him a kingdom, and then condemning him?

2. Consider Ahijah (14:13); he pleased God in some way, and so died peacefully while still a child. What bearing may this have on questions about the position of children who die?

3. Baasha's *might* (16:5) suggests his twenty-four year rule was not without some success, yet he was totally condemned. Think about your career in the light of Baasha's and of Luke 12:13–21.

4. Stories such as Elijah and the widow of Zarephath are often treated as fables or folk-lore and not as historical or factual accounts. Does it matter to you if these events did not really happen? Why, or why not?

20 Ahab and his enemy

Ahab's was an eventful reign. This chapter tells of conflict with Damascus, the dominant power in southern Syria in the mid-ninth century BC. Ben-hadad headed an alliance of thirty-two kings, probably formed to resist pressure from Assyria in the north-east. Assyria fought Ben-hadad, Israel, and their allies in 853 BC at Qarqar on the Orontes, both Damascus and Israel submitting to Assyria in 841 for a few years.

Ben-hadad, heading his coalition, apparently aimed to coerce Ahab into an alliance by besieging Samaria; with Ahab would have come Judah and Moab. Ahab readily sent his submission to his enemy in accepted diplomatic terms. Ben-hadad pressed for their literal performance then added, in effect, the surrender of the capital for looting by his army.

Ahab, supported by the people, for Israel was not a dictatorship, resisted, provoking Ben-hadad's arrogant claim (10) and the warning reply that the time for boasting is after the battle (11). Ahab found further support in prophetic guidance. It was quite a small force that came out of the city, taking advantage of the warmest time of day, catching the Syrians unready. Only rebuffed, Ben-hadad's officers planned another campaign, the combined armies under unified control. A good excuse was found for the first defeat, dictating the new strategy; they had not realised the reality of Israel's God compared with the illusion they worshipped (23). Ahab had overcome on the first occasion, spurred to react against Ben-hadad's arrogance. Now his victory would result from the Syrian scorn of God, again bringing home to him the lesson that Elijah had already brought (28, compare 18:36,37).

The tables turned and Ahab treated Ben-hadad as an equal as readily as he had submitted to him before. Yet his humanity to his enemy earned God's condemnation, depicted with a stark reminder of the perils which disobeying God's word brings. Ahab could have served God by executing the foreign king who had belittled him. His clemency eventually brought him back into conflict with Ben-hadad, and to his death.

Notes: On the numbers (29,30), see the *Introduction* to Chronicles. The wives and families of conquered kings, and their treasures (3), were commonly seized by the conqueror.

THOUGHTS: Israel's army waited seven days to vindicate God's name, and in what a position (27)! God claims the right to vengeance but may instruct his servants to carry it out. What lessons can you learn from the relationship of Ahab and Ben-hadad?

21 Ahab's folly

Elijah had fled when Jezebel heard of his triumph on Mount Carmel (19:1–3); Naboth had no escape when Jezebel heard what Ahab wanted. Here the attitude of those ruled by illusion (ch. 18) is demonstrated: if Ahab wanted something, then he should have it, no matter how. Note the stages of the story: Ahab's demand was rejected (2,3) so he sulked childishly, drawing the queen's attention. Jezebel took the authority of the king's name and seal, caused the leaders of Jezreel to work with criminals for the murder of the innocent, and the whole populace carried out the stoning, as required by Leviticus 24:16. The execution could not have been more public nor, apparently, more readily taken in hand by the people. How seriously did the charge of blasphemy weigh with the Israelites who so recently had been 'limping with two different opinions' (18:21)?

With Naboth dead, Jezebel thought Ahab could claim the property; there is evidence that a criminal's property was forfeit to the crown in other ancient societies. Ahab knew this did not hold in Israel; the land remained in its owner's family (see Lev. 25). Yet his greed drove all else from his mind until Elijah met him. Then Ahab's conscience spoke at once, *my enemy*, contrast 18:17. The prophet's words struck home and Ahab's reactions evinced not merely self-pity but repentance when faced with the doom of his dynasty, so God could show mercy. However wicked, Ahab had not used his power to kill Naboth or sieze his land in the first instance.

Did Elijah alone object to the crime, or did Jezebel's letter cow the Jezreelites into connivance? Or had idolatry so demoralised them that they did not care, nor object to testimony from known *base fellows*? When the powerful pervert justice, the man of God must speak. Amos, Hosea and many other prophets who were not afraid to speak against the kings of their times followed Elijah's example. Although Israel was privileged to have God's laws, notice that it was a royal duty to uphold justice in all ancient states, so Jezebel's action would have been widely condemned. In other states, however, it was the king who made and altered the laws, as parliaments and congresses do today. God's laws are immutable with a standard that is so high men want to replace them, ignoring the fact that the Creator should be trusted to know what is best for his creatures.

THOUGHT: How alert are you to character assassination? Do you demonstrate its falsity when you see it, or do you go along with the crowd, cowed by the majority opinion or world authorities?

22:1–40 Ahab's fall

Despite the pact of 20:34, disputes remained between Syria and Israel. After a united front brought some relief from Assyrian pressure in 853 BC, Ahab felt able to press his claim to Ramoth-gilead, which was probably in the region of Er-ramtha, now the frontier post of Jordan with Syria. Was he seeking aggrandisement, or trying to impress the king of Judah?

As so often in the Old Testament, the story gives an example of what was a common practice: divine guidance was sought before a military expedition began. The southern king, Ahab's junior ally (4, see 20:4) insisted on the inquiry, and the prophets spoke in the name of the Lord, not of Baal. Yet Jehoshaphat perceived they were Ahab's men; Ahab preferred the illusory comfort the four hundred gave him to the reality he feared to hear from Micaiah. The prophet's first words (15) were evidently spoken in such a way that Ahab recognised they were not to be taken at face value.

Micaiah's vision enables the story to be seen both from God's side and from man's. The 'lying spirit' permitted to entice Ahab would encourage him to do what he wanted to do. Yet the possibility of escape existed; the very revelation of the scene in the heavenly court established it. As always, God does not permit temptation without an alternative. Ahab rejected Micaiah, as God had known he would, holding him in prison to await his victory. Deuteronomy 18:20–22 gives the common-sense basis for Micaiah's response.

Ahab feared that Micaiah's words were true, so he tried to nullify them by his disguise, not caring about added risk this might give Jehoshaphat. The Syrian archer thought he shot at random; Micaiah's vision reveals that the arrow's flight was pre-determined. The truth was inescapable but Ahab acted at the last as a king (35). Syria's king knew the war was Ahab's personal project, hence the order of v. 31.

Note: *the ivory house* (39) was not built of ivory but lavishly decorated with it as veneer or panelling on the walls and furniture. Fragments found in the palace at Samaria are in the British Museum and, principally, in the Rockefeller Museum in Jerusalem. For illustrations see *IBD* pp. 1375, 1378.

THOUGHT: Four hundred prophets told the king what he wanted to hear; only time could show if they were right. Read 1 John 4:1–3 for further criteria.

22:41–2 **Kings 1:**18
Is there no God in Israel?

Although a good king, Jehoshaphat's reign has only a brief record here (compare 2 Chron. 17–20). The aims and interests of the compilers of Kings probably account for this. His refusal to allow Israel any share in his expedition to Ophir may have arisen from his experience at Ramoth-gilead.

Ahab's son Ahaziah learnt nothing from his father's experiences. Ahab learnt that he might compel a prophet to come to him, but he could not be sure he would speak the word of God (22:9–16). Now Ahaziah found that the man of God would only come to him at his own time, God's time. God would only speak through him in his time, too. The stricken man badly wanted divine guidance but from a pagan god, again despite the lessons of Ahab's life. Thus he insulted the God of his people. Nevertheless, he recognised the authority and power of Elijah, as did his messengers. His captain and men presumably went to arrest the prophet, or bring him under escort. Elijah's reply (10) suggests that their words and manner were disrespectful, even mocking. The reply has the emphasis on the 'If' to contrast the power of God with human arms. The third captain had learnt his lesson (13,14). Elijah need not fear him. Even so, the prophet only went with him at the angel's command. He approached the king directly: he would die and the reason is clear. Ahaziah may have heard that the god of Ekron had special healing powers, as some ancient gods were reputed to have, but he should have known that the God of Israel, who rules every aspect of life, could even heal him, let alone answer his inquiry.

He died as a result of his act and caused the deaths of 102 of his soldiers, a reminder of the effects of one man's sin (compare Achan and the deaths at Ai, Josh. 7:1–5,11,12; Adam, Rom. 5:12–14). As king he was responsible, but clearly failed to reckon life as precious. By his plea, the third captain showed he knew where the power over life and death truly lay.

Notes: *Baal-zebub* means 'lord of flies' and may be a distortion by pious scribes of the name Baal-zebul, 'prince Baal' (as in Matt. 12:24) to avoid writing the pagan name. *The lattice* (2) was a window covering, still seen in old Turkish houses, used in place of glass.

THOUGHT: What premium should we place on human life? Does the Christian value people's lives more than the rest of the world does? If so, what should he or she do about it?

2:1–18 Elijah and Elisha

Like Moses, Elijah left this world in an unusual way, more obviously taken to God than other men, indicating his special status in God's service. The manner of Elijah's going defies explanation, but that does not mean it is impossible; it is worth noting that an extensive search failed to discover his body.

Elijah knew he was about to leave this world, yet his treatment of Elisha is ambiguous. Did he want to be alone? Was he testing his disciple's faithfulness to see if he would desert him for continuing service elsewhere? Elisha's stubbornness was evidently right, he was not easily dissuaded. At each stage he was given an opportunity to leave Elijah, until they came to the barrier of the Jordan. (The whole journey was about twenty-five to thirty miles, forty to forty-eight km.) As on earlier occasions, those determined to do God's will found that physical obstacles could be removed, so now the two men crossed dry-shod. Again, inability to understand or explain the event in scientific terms should not lead to a sceptical attitude to the account. In fact, the flow of the Jordan has stopped in medieval and in modern times in the region of Jericho as a result of cliffs falling and blocking the river bed further up-stream.

The 'double share' which Elisha requested was the share of the heir in his father's estate (Deut. 21:17). If this was granted there would be no doubt Elisha was Elijah's successor, even if he did not possess the whole of Elijah's powers. How great those seemed to the younger man is seen in his cry; Elijah was of more importance to Israel than the whole of the nation's army (compare 13:14).

Elijah's mantle carried its owner's prestige and perhaps some distinctive mark. Elisha used it to find out if he had truly succeeded Elijah. His question does not throw doubt on God's existence, as Elijah's implied that Ahaziah had done (1:3 etc.); it is the cry of faith that seeks assurance. Elisha needed to know before he met others who might ask him for a public display. Without assurance, he could not act as God's spokesman.

It would seem that groups or bands of prophets roamed Israel, using their gifts as required. Here they plainly recognise the higher status of Elijah and Elisha (contrast 1 Kings 22:24–28).

THOUGHT: Consider, as a model for your life, Elisha's determination to follow his master. Compare John 11:16; 13:36–38; Revelation 2:26–28.

2:19–3:27 The prophet's deeds

Elisha's first action was entirely practical, to relieve the plight of Jericho. The city had been derelict until shortly before (1 Kings 16:34), which may explain the polluted water-supply. Again, the story stresses the unbreakable link of every part of life to the spiritual realm. By dropping salt into the spring, the prophet symbolically 'seasoned' the water and removed the curse that lay on the city (compare Josh. 6:26), so that those who used the spring could enjoy God's blessings.

The second action rouses strong feelings among modern readers; what a terrible punishment for a moment's boyish rudeness! Is it a 'puerile tale', or is it a lesson in respect for God and his servants? Israel had learnt of God's power and holiness, or should have done, through the events of Ahab's reign; yet here were youngsters whose parents had failed to teach them a true sense of values. They were like the first two sets of soldiers in ch. 1. Whether the lads were seven year-olds or in their early teens, they were still under parental authority and their deaths punished their parents as well. There is no indication that baldness was a mark of a prophet.

Elisha's third reported act involved the nation. Moab had been subject to Israel, but Mesha tells in his own inscription (the Moabite Stone) how he shook off Israel's yoke. Edom was subject to Israel, with a king appointed by the suzerain, so had to join the campaign (see 1 Kings 22:47). Jehoshaphat was again drawn into Israel's adventures and again sought God's advice. When Elisha spoke, it was for Jehoshaphat's sake and he said more than the kings expected; they would win a total victory. The water apparently came as a flash flood from the hills of Edom, the morning sun falling on the sudden accumulation deluding the Moabites so that they were easy prey. Israel's devastation of Moab exceeds the directions of Deuteronomy 20 because she was crushing a rebellion. Despite the victory, the end was abrupt. Moab's king took an extreme step in sacrificing his son. The *great wrath* has puzzled commentators. Many see it as being a disaster (akin to that following Achan's sin – Josh. 22:20) which Israel superstitiously attributed to the power of Moab's god. Others think Israel withdrew in a reaction of horror, a feeling that her attack had gone too far.

Note: 3:15 literally reads: 'whenever the minstrel played', implying a common practice.

THOUGHT: Notice Elisha's reputation (3:12). What do people say of you?

4 Elisha gives help

Here are four accounts of the power of God working through his servant to ease the trials of people loyal to him. The first can be compared with Elijah and the widow of Zarephath (1 Kings 17), but the circumstances are quite different. Had misfortune or bad housekeeping brought one of the prophetic group into debt? Oil was a basic requirement, easy for the widow to sell. What she received was as much as she could cope with, sufficient for her immediate relief and for the future. Elisha was absent when the miracle occurred, he was merely God's agent.

With the Shunammite woman the prophet had a long-standing relationship. Her hospitality was rewarded, then the reward seemed to be snatched from her. Like Abraham when his promised son was demanded from him (Gen. 22), she trusted that he would be restored and rode some twenty miles from her home north of Jezreel to the man of God, despite her husband's objections. Elisha sent Gehazi ahead to prepare for his coming and to report the situation to him. Later, even with Elisha's staff Gehazi could effect nothing; the prophet's prayer of faith was essential. By resting on the boy, Elisha identified himself with him, so life was transferred to the lifeless by divine power. This was not an easy miracle accomplished by a simple touch or word (35). It was, again, a private affair.

The third and fourth incidents concern food for the prophetic bands. The wild gourds were probably cucumber-like colocynths, bitter tasting, purgative in effect, and poisonous in large quantity. In famine everything possible will be used for food. Elisha's flour may have absorbed or countered the poison, more likely it was a symbolic act, as in 2:21. At Baal-shalisha in the plain of Sharon, Elisha accepted a moderate gift of first-fruits as a servant of God with no other livelihood, and provided from it enough food for 100 men. Once more the servant's poor faith, the prophet's confidence and God's abundant provision, are evident.

THOUGHT: The widow's words, 'Your servant feared the Lord', and the Shunammite's, 'Did I ask my lord for a son?' seem to reproach God. What is the Christian reaction to adversity?

Questions for further study and discussion on 1 Kings 20–2 Kings 4

1. The scene in heaven in 1 Kings 22 is unusual. Many find it difficult to accommodate the account within their concept of God as Truth. Can you explain it to your satisfaction? How, or why not?

2. The Syrians had a very localised concept of God (20:23), yet the Israelites hardly recognised the extent of his power. The victory they gained was for a specific purpose (20:28). What role does this purpose play in other parts of the Bible? What place does it have in Christian life today?

3. Can the character of the God of Elijah, seen in 2 Kings 1, be reconciled with the picture of God in the New Testament?

4. May Elisha's cure of Jericho's spring (2 Kings 2) be used as an analogy for Christian involvement in human well-being? Does this story give any guidance for the manner of such actions?

5. Look up the laws about caring for the needy (eg. Exod. 22:21–27; Deut. 14:28,29). Elisha's help reached people in every part of society who had needs they could not meet themselves (kings, towns, a debtor). How alert are you to needs in your circle of acquaintances, and how do you identify them and try to meet them?

5 Israel's God heals a foreign general

This famous story contrasts a pagan general with a prophet's servant, pride with humility, generosity with greed. Naaman may have commanded at Ramoth-gilead (1 Kings 22). His victory was the work of Israel's God, according to the Israelite historian, although the Syrian would have said it was his god, Rimmon's. In the same way, he would think of his illness as coming from Rimmon and doubtless had sought to be healed by praying and making gifts to him. His disease, 'leprosy', had not led to his exclusion from society; it was plainly a non-contagious form, probably progressive, with the threat of disability and eventual ostracism (compare Azariah, 15:5).

The foreign general could not approach the Israelite prophet directly but, in observing diplomatic propriety, the king of Damascus failed to make his purpose clear. The king of Israel was at fault, also, in his reaction; the slave-girl knew exactly who could help. Elisha's readiness to save the day was almost negated by his apparently off-hand attitude to Naaman in only sending a message to him. Naaman expected a prophet to conduct a formal ceremony, calling for God's help; he did not expect instructions for a bath! His servants followed the helpful path of his wife's maid, so allowing God's power to be displayed. Pre-scientific age men more readily saw God's hand at work than we do; Naaman had no doubt that Elisha's God had healed him, he owed him his life. Elisha refused a reward, for his part was secondary. His needs were supplied by God and he could not let Naaman think he had purchased his cure, or that the matter could be settled and forgotten through a gift given. It was to mark the rest of Naaman's life. He could assure the general that God would respect his worship despite the appearances his duty demanded. No one should judge those who find themselves in a comparable position.

The servant Gehazi misread his master's act and hoped to salvage something for himself. His folly was compounded by his lying in Elisha's name. Like Achan and Judas, he was discovered and condemned before he could enjoy his gain. His sentence was to live with the disease whose cure Naaman won by obedience.

Notes: *the Abana river* is the Barada whose clear waters still flow through modern Damascus, whereas the Jordan is muddy. *Verse 26:* Elisha enlarges on the scope of Gehazi's gain to drive home his point.

THOUGHT: The Israelite captive exemplifies Matthew 5:44. Translate this into political and social terms for today: In what practical ways can we live out this command?

6:1–23 Elisha at work

The account of the floating axe-head is commonly labelled folk-lore – the prophet with common sense, probing to find the axe then fishing it out with a stick, later becoming a tale of miracle. Yet Elisha's action is clearly described (6) and although the mechanism is hidden, the miracle answered the need which a desperate man's faith led him to lay before the man of God. It should not be lightly dismissed.

In saving his people from slaughter, although they remained open to attack from Damascus, Elisha demonstrated that he possessed the most distinctive quality of Elijah (2:12). Despite the nation's spiritual malaise, God continued to speak through his servant to the king of Israel. This was probably Joram, Ahab's son, who had at least broken with Baal (3:2). Elisha's inspired advice was purely practical, for that is as much within God's concern as the spiritual. Not surprisingly, the Aramean was frustrated, yet his aides knew what was going on, another sign of Elisha's repute. Israel's weakness was plain, for Dothan lay only about ten miles (sixteen km.) north of Samaria and the *strong force* of Syrians could march there. Elisha's servant saw the physical threat and was afraid; Elisha knew the spiritual forces and prayed. His prayer was not for himself, or for safety, but for his servant to be shown the reality upon which his own faith rested. If he was to go to the king of Syria, it would be at God's time (compare ch. 1). Now the servant had his spiritual eyes open to realise the battle was not confined to human levels (compare Eph. 6:12). God answered Elisha's second prayer and physically blinded Syria's soldiers. The blindness is described with a word only used otherwise of the men of Sodom in Genesis 19:11. Modern science might explain it as a form of mass hysteria. Utterly helpless, the Syrians followed Elisha. Captives who had not fought should not be slaughtered, he said, for a slaughter might provoke further attacks and would obscure the evidence of God's power over a strong enemy. The good treatment was effective (23 end, compare 2 Chron. 28).

Each of these incidents has a man turning to Elisha with the words, *Alas, my lord* (5,15). The prophet replied to each, the first by direct action, the second by prayer. In each case the man of God was ready and able to respond to the need and bring relief.

THOUGHT: Study the words and actions of the man of God.

6:24–7:20 Samaria saved

Syria continued to fight for supremacy over Israel. Her forces encircled the capital this time. The king blamed Elisha, we may assume, because he had let the Syrians go home unharmed earlier. The elders looked to the prophet for God's guidance, and he may have foretold relief already. Meanwhile, the siege led people to extremes, eating unclean food and even turning to cannibalism, extremes not unknown in wars since. They are usually the result of man's inhumanity to man. Even so, there were some who made money with their inflated prices.

The king initially told the distraught woman that only God could help, perhaps speaking in a flippant way, but then proposed to kill the man who spoke for God. It is notable that Elisha was in the city sharing its straits, so was able to promise help. The king's attitude changed, but only to ask, with many who lack faith, Why does God not act *now*? The wait is never due to impotence on God's part; yet when he does speak the cynical and sceptical treat his word as the captain treated Elisha's – as ridiculous.

The sequel is vividly related. As the reader anticipates divine intervention, four lepers enter the story. Even during the siege they remained outside the city and so they could scout around the Syrian camp. As for Naaman, so for Samaria: the good news came through those society disregarded. Although they were diseased, unclean, their message brought life to the city (compare 1 Cor. 1:27–29). They had reached the depths where they thought they were only choosing the manner of their inevitable death. At that point God stepped in, causing the enemy to panic. The king's suspicions are understandable (7:12). Not so the faithless captain, who evidently did not accept Elisha as God's spokesman; he learnt too late that God does act for his people, in his way and at his time.

Notes: *dove's dung* (6:25) could be meant literally as food or as fuel, or be a plant – perhaps the carob. The amount (1 *cab*) was about half a litre. Elisha may have used the term *this murderer* inasmuch as the king planned murder, but the Hebrew text reads 'son of a murderer', which could refer to Ahab. The kings of the *Hittites* (7:6) ruled small states in Syria and southern Turkey, and were to be found in various alliances for and against Damascus.

THOUGHT: This is a day of good news; what right have we to be silent?

8:1–24 Politics

The first section (1–8) refers to the Shunammite of ch. 4 in the context of Gehazi's recital of his master's deeds. The story does not assume Elisha's death, rather it belongs to the time before Gehazi contracted Naaman's leprosy. In the face of Elisha's prophecy, the woman left her property; it may be that her husband was alive then but died during their stay in Philistia. Returning, she had to prove her claim to the land, now she was a widow. As a living evidence of Elisha's great deeds, she deserved the provision the un-named king gave to her.

After the hostile relations between Israel and Syria, Elisha's interference in Syria may seem strange. Once more the control of God over the affairs of other nations is declared and the commission to Elijah (1 Kings 19:15) is at last fulfilled. Ben-hadad took advantage of Elisha's visit, perhaps knowing of Naaman's cure but failing to learn about payment. The prophet's interview with Hazael is problematic. His words seem to be deliberately misleading until it is realised that Elisha foresees Ben-hadad's death but does not attribute it to his illness. Rather, the prophet's fixed gaze and tears indicate his reading of Hazael's character and his potential to bring evil both on his own Syrian king and on the people of Israel. Even as Elisha spoke more of the future may have been revealed to him. Hazael's reply uses a common ancient form of self-abasement, the dog having no value in ancient society. Returning to his own master, he made sure there was not enough time for him to recover his strength lest he be deprived of his prospect. Assyrian inscriptions record Hazael's rule in Damascus, making it clear he was a usurper ('a son of nobody').

Jehoshaphat's son exposed the folly of his father's alliance with Israel. Married to Ahab's daughter, Jehoram brought Jezebel's influence into Judah. His power declined; Edom was lost – a valuable source of income – as was the town of Libnah. Only his ancestor's qualities saved Judah from greater calamities.

Through all these political moves, the prophet Elisha sustained God's truth, demonstrating his impartiality and, it appears, carrying out his commands without question, despite their danger to his own country. His reputation rested on the way God used him and the fact that he allowed God to use him.

THOUGHT: Does the thought of man's evil to man make us weep? Does the constant display of violence in the media harden us to it? How is Isaiah 42:3 relevant?

8:25–9:37 Ahab's dynasty ended

Ahaziah continued to impose on Judah the heritage of Jezebel and, like Jehoshaphat, joined Israel in a frontier war to hold Ramoth-gilead (9:14). While the two kings were away from the theatre of war, Elisha set events in motion to end Ahab's line and its pagan attitudes. Elisha's messenger was to act in secret. His addition to Elisha's words may have come to him through inspiration (Jehu's friends saw him in a state of ecstasy, 'this mad fellow' 9:11), or been given by his master. By running off he escaped curious questioning and gossip; Jehu's report was to his fellow commanders. Had they been plotting already, or was the prophetic anointing and oracle sufficient for them to raise Jehu above them?

Secrecy and speed were vital. Jehu had no doubt he was to assassinate his king. As he advanced swiftly he detained the king's messengers, hoping to learn of a victory at Ramoth-gilead, lest they learn of the plot. (Reading this story, remember a chariot would probably travel at most at twelve miles, twenty kilometres, per hour and so be visible for some time coming up the valley to Jezreel.) Joram and Ahaziah hurried to discover what was afoot. Jehu's acid response, alluding to Jezebel's pagan practices, gave all the answer they needed. The meeting-place was significant, as Jehu remarked. Ahaziah tried to escape along the road to Judah, then sought refuge in the north-west at Megiddo.

Jezebel was Ahab's evil genius and never gave up hope of ensnaring the man in power. Her call to Jehu was a taunt, for Zimri lasted only seven days (1 Kings 16:10–18) after destroying the ruling house. Was there a hint of invitation in her question, 'Is it peace'? The special effects (30) did not impress Jehu, even the eunuchs thought the queen worthless! Jehu's eating simply stresses his contempt for Jezebel.

Notes: *She was a daughter of Omri* is the literal Hebrew of 8:26, but 'daughter' can mean a female descendant. *Harlotries and sorceries* (9:22) could be figurative terms, but are as likely to be meant literally, alluding to the fertility cults and magic inherited from the Canaanites.

THOUGHT: Ahab's marriage to Jezebel may have had political advantages; in every other way it was wrong. How can the Christian balance all considerations in making a decision; and which criteria should be dominant?

10 Jehu's zeal

The death of Ahab's wife and son was insufficient to cleanse Israel; the whole of his family and all connected with Jezebel's heathen religion had to be exterminated. Jehu moved carefully, testing the leaders of the royal cities and the custodians of the royal family to see if they would support a king of Ahab's line. Leaderless, they changed sides and murdered their charges. Heads of criminals and traitors adorned public gates in London until the eighteenth century as a sign of justice done and as a warning. Jezreel's gruesome sight testified to Jehu's policy, he followed a common custom. His morning speech to the people opens with a puzzling clause, 'You are innocent' (RSV, NIV) or 'righteous' (RV). An assurance may be intended that no general slaughter will follow, or that they are free from any blame. Alternatively, Jehu may have claimed all was the work of God. Better is the understanding that Jehu admits his treachery, but expects the 'righteous' people will realise that the whole series of unsavoury events was to fulfil the Lord's purpose.

To obtain the throne Jehu had acted upon Elisha's inspiration. To return Israel to the worship of her own God he had the aid of the puritanical and orthodox Jehonadab (compare Jer. 35 for Rechabite tenets). After Jehu's assertions of loyalty to the Lord, his proposed worship of Baal may have sounded odd to the Baalists, yet they came. Jehu's invitation (18,19) was deliberately ambiguous, the 'great sacrifice' would comprise Baal's adherents. The massacre offends as a cruel extreme, yet what else could Jehu have done? Certainly his work received divine approval, though with a limitation (30) and with no promise of greatness. Yet even as God's agent, Jehu's deeds called forth a reproach, see Hosea 1:4. Hazael of Damascus continued Ben-hadad's aim to control northern Transjordan with its rich pastures and forests.

Note: *the pillar* (26) was a symbol of the god's presence; it could be stone or wood. Jehu is known from a famous Assyrian monument, the Black Obelisk of Shalmaneser III, which shows him or his messenger bowing before the Assyrian king, with a team of porters carrying precious pieces of plate as tribute. He is described as 'Jehu of the house of Omri'.

THOUGHT: Jehu's zeal (16) fell short (31). How many Christian leaders or enterprises, local or world-wide, fail to achieve as much as they could? Why is this? (See, eg. 1 Cor. 3:5–15.)

11:1–12:16 Reform in Judah

Athaliah, seeing no chance of ruling Judah through a new king, perhaps because the court would have been against her, determined to eradicate the line of David, and rule herself. A ruling queen was a rarity, though not unknown in the ancient Near East. Her daughter, or half-daughter, thwarted her by saving one small grandson. Clearly there was a staunchly anti-Baal party in Jerusalem and it grew under Athaliah's unpopular régime, as persecuted groups often do.

Jehoiada, high priest of the temple, led the plot to restore the kingship to David's line. He timed it to give him the greatest military support so that his protégé should not be at risk. Even so, he had to fall back on antique weapons to arm his supporters (10). His move proved popular. Athaliah, the last of Ahab's family, had to die, her execution being carefully arranged to avoid defiling the temple. As in much Old Testament history writing, the vivid narrative switches from one scene to another and back again (15,16,20). Joash was crowned in the proper manner and given the 'testimony', which was probably God's covenant with Israel (compare 1 Sam. 10:25). The pillar he stood by was at the doorway (2 Chron. 23:13), perhaps *Jachin* or *Boaz*, visible to the people. With the king duly installed, the priest secured the loyalty of his subjects to God's covenant and to the king as God's anointed ruler. Solemnised as 'the Lord's people', they were compelled to rid the capital of Baal worship. The result of putting things right was rejoicing.

Joash wanted things done properly, and when he found they were not, took steps to ensure they were. The priests had come to regard all money gifts as their perquisite; now they were limited to what was rightly theirs and the rest was applied to the restoration work.

Note: *Carites* (11:4) were mercenary soldiers from southern Turkey. *Acquaintance* (12:5) could also be translated 'assessor'.

THOUGHT: In churches as in society, once a clear lead is given, people are as ready to do what they know is right as to do wrong. Do Christians leave their churches and their society to wait for a Jehoiada, or do they assert the proper way?

Questions for further study and discussion on 2 Kings 5–12:16

1. When you feel disheartened, thinking there is nothing you can do for God, or that he cannot use you, remember the role of the Israelite girl in Naaman's house. What similar cases can you find in scripture? What do they teach about God's ways?

2. Outline the course of Israel's relations with Damascus. Is there a pattern in it, or is it a random sequence of victories and defeats? If you were a Syrian, how would you trace the power of the God of Israel at work?

3. Why did God give Elisha a commission to the Arameans that would harm Israel?

4. Ahab and Jezebel left a legacy of paganism and violence, but Jehu was little better. Did Israel deserve such rulers (note Rom. 13:1)? Why, or why not?

Despite the good of Joash, he suffered the attacks of the ambitious Hazael of Damascus whom he bought off with the material splendour of the temple and the palace. 2 Chronicles 24:17–22 explains how Joash went astray after his mentor Jehoiada had died; his change of policy may have provoked his assassination. His son promised to follow the pattern of his father's earlier years (14:3).

In Israel Jehu's son followed his father's ways, failing to take the major step to bring Israel back to orthodoxy. He only understood military defeat. Hazael and his son, no longer attacking Judah, pressed Israel hard. Worn down, Jehoahaz came to understand he could not trust his own abilities (his power had gone, 13:7) and, as so many do, he turned to God as his last resort. God's response demonstrated his mercy (13:23). The *saviour* (13:5) was perhaps Elisha, or the Assyrian king Adad-nirari III who defeated Hazael about 800 BC.

Jehoash, or Joash of Israel took advantage of the weakness of Damascus and advanced, but could not press the advantage home. Elisha, dying, offered the king an occasion to show his faith in *the Lord's arrow of victory*. Despite respecting the prophet as Israel's true strength, the king's restraint showed too little faith. Unless complete and continuous, faith is fruitless.

Elisha left no named successor. Other true prophets did arise soon afterwards (Jonah, 14:25, Amos and Hosea), for God did not leave his people without his spokesman. Yet even after death, Elisha could vitalise another man. This sounds like a folk-story and its meaning is unclear, but it should not be rejected, for God's power is not limited. Although the man's friends deserted him, God did not!

In Judah, the new king acted according to the Law (Deut. 24:16), yet his first victory went to his head, as Jehoash warned him. Jerusalem was left defenceless and impoverished, Amaziah was disgraced to perish in another conspiracy. His son Azariah, also known as Uzziah, followed the conquest of Edom by opening the port of Elath to trade.

Israel attained its greatest power under Jeroboam II, controlling the area from central Syria to the Dead Sea. The following prosperity led to the excesses condemned by Amos and Hosea.

Note: *had belonged to Judah* (14:28): Damascus and Hamath belonged to Judah during the reigns of David and Solomon.

THOUGHT: How often do we follow Amaziah in disdaining the parable of the thistle?

15 Israel in decline

Azariah, also known as Uzziah, was a good king, yet he had leprosy. The author of Kings states 'the Lord smote the king'; 2 Chronicles 26:16–21 explains why: he had become proud. His long reign was roughly contemporary with Jeroboam II's in Israel, and both kingdoms prospered at a time when other powers, notably Assyria, were less active. The death of Azariah marked an outstanding moment in the career of the prophet Isaiah (Isa. 6:1).

Israel's history after the death of Jeroboam II is a tale of decline and disaster. Zechariah could not command as his father had done, or suffered a reaction against his father's policies. His death was 'at Ibleam' according to some of the Greek versions, where Jehu had killed the king of Judah. The usurper, Shallum, lasted only a month, falling to Menahem's sword. The new king, determined to hold power, dealt brutally with a town that did not welcome him. His power was curtailed as Assyria rose under Pul, better known as Tiglath-pileser III, re-asserting his control of Syria-Palestine. Menahem paid tribute, making Israel a vassal-state of Assyria; everyone of substance was directly involved through the poll-tax. Pekahiah continued his father's ways and was murdered by his captain, Pekah. Assyria did not accept the change of ruler and captured the north of the country. The deportation of people from the land led to impoverishment for the country and less nationalistic support for the native rulers. It was an ancient policy revived by Pul. Assyria then encouraged Hoshea to take the throne. This series of power struggles and murders weakened the state and revealed the lack of firm moral basis and leadership in society.

In Judah another 'good' king arose, Jotham, yet he was attacked by Pekah and the king of Edom. Their reasons were probably political, to force Judah to league with them against Assyria. The historian states that 'the Lord sent them' without explanation.

Notes: *a separate house* (5); this was to avoid infecting others. Verses 19,20: with a talent of 3,000 shekels, the tax indicates there were 60,000 'wealthy men' in Israel at this time. Fifty shekels seems to have been the average price of a slave.

THOUGHT: Israel's sins, it is implied, brought Assyria's attacks. Was the attack on Judah a similar punishment, or a test of faith? How should churches and individual Christians react to attacks and reverses?

16 The weakness of Ahaz of Judah

There is no guarantee that a godly father or family will produce a godly son. Ahaz is a clear example of that. His little kingdom of Judah was threatened by two states that appeared to be much stronger, and to his mind there was only one place he could go for help, the only stronger human power, Assyria. Isaiah told him the right place to seek salvation (Isa. 7), but he persisted in going his own, wrong way, calling in a greater evil to destroy a smaller. Perhaps vainly trying to fend off the besiegers, he descended to the depths of paganism, burning his son as a sacrifice (compare 2 Kings 3:27; Jer. 19:5 shows this rite continued later in Judah). Ahaz not only subjected his people to the worship of alien gods, he brought them under the yoke of an alien king. Tiglath-pileser's depredations in Israel had brought Assyria close to Judah, and Judah's attackers probably wanted her support in an attempt to drive Assyria back. Ahaz hoped to trap them by an Assyrian attack in the rear, while he was safe under the Assyrian umbrella. Damascus duly fell to the Assyrians in 732 BC. Ahaz' policy cost Judah dear. Although Assyria left loyal vassals to run their own affairs, subject to the treaty setting up the relationship, she demanded regular payments of tribute. Ahaz had first of all to buy Assyrian help with the temple treasures and his own. It may have been partly to meet Assyria's demands that he took the bronze work from the temple furnishings (17), while demolishing the special entrance, presumably as a sign of his vassal status. Ahaz's new altar need not have been a symbol of subjection, as many have supposed, but a new or different style that appealed to the king. By commanding the innovation, Ahaz set himself above the orthodox ritual which was derived from Mosaic law, and so against its Author.

THOUGHT: Read Isaiah 7 beside this chapter. Ahaz could only see the immediate threat and a possible solution in his own terms. 'If you will not believe, surely you shall not be established.'

17 Israel's end

Hoshea failed his Assyrian masters. A dutiful subject at first, he fell to Egypt's blandishments and stopped paying his annual tribute to Assyria. This was rebellion. Assyria's forces advanced in punishment. Hoshea was dethroned and Samaria besieged for three years. Shalmaneser V of Assyria began the operation, the city fell in 722 BC, and the deportation was carried out by the next king of Assyria, Sargon II. The deportees found new homes in north-east Syria (Gozan), east of Nineveh (Halah), and in western Iran (Media). All were far from their own land. In their place the Assyrians settled other conquered peoples, who brought their own pagan concepts with them. Ravaged by lions, emboldened by the reduction in human activity, the new inhabitants of Samaria rightly assumed that the God whose land they occupied was angry. Although their view of God was limited, it still had some truth in it. So worship of the true God was re-established at Bethel. Regrettably, the priest's teaching was defective, or not accepted, for the monotheism of orthodox Israel was ignored. God was made one of many, set beside the local gods the settlers brought from their homelands. Ultimately, the Samaritans were descended from this mixture and they continued to be candidates for God's mercy (John 4:39–42). Lions still roamed in Palestine in the time of the Crusades.

Verses 7–23 contain the historian's meditation on the fall of Israel. Whatever role politics may have played, the real causes were moral and religious. What God had done for Israel to bring her into being was overlooked. His patient, continuing warnings were unheeded; less severe punishments had only momentary effects. The kings and the people followed the illusion that they could make their own way, with their own ideas of God and their own standards. They, and the world, had to be shown that man cannot rule himself; God's justice had to be satisfied. The nation as a whole was punished, virtually destroyed, for its apostasy; but the blame did not rest on the nation as a vague entity, it was the responsibility of each man and woman who belonged to the nation. So Israel was removed. Judah was allowed a longer period of grace (13,18) and had the example of Israel as a warning.

THOUGHT: Israel forfeited the land God had promised, they 'did secretly . . . things that were not right' (verse 9), they went after false gods and so became false (verse 15). Check the way you live with Ephesians 5:3–20.

18;19 Hezekiah and Sennacherib (1)

This amazing story has to be read at a sitting. Judah's good kings had given place to weak Ahaz, then his son, Hezekiah, brought back 'good' and surpassed his ancestors. Where Ahaz had relied on Assyria for relief from Syrian and Israelite attacks, his son relied on God for relief from Assyria's attacks. Hezekiah seems to have determined that his people should owe allegiance to God alone in politics and in religion.

Hezekiah's rebellion began about the time of the death of Sargon of Assyria (*c*.705 BC), when there was opportunity to support anti-Assyrian movements in Philistia which that king had conquered (see Isaiah 20). The new Assyrian king, Sennacherib, had other rebels to suppress before he could march west. In 701 BC he 'came down like a wolf on the fold'. Hezekiah, as a rebellious vassal, through his father's pact, had to be punished. With all his cities taken except the capital, Hezekiah paid the heavy fine imposed by the Assyrian. What happened next is much debated by scholars. From verse 17 to 19:37 is the account of Sennacherib's attempt to talk Jerusalem into submission, and of the salvation of the city. Mention of Tirhakah (19:9) led many to assume this account refers to a later campaign by Sennacherib, about 688 BC, after Tirhakah became pharaoh. New evidence implies that Tirhakah could have led an army in 701 BC. So it appears that the account continues after Hezekiah's payment with no interval. Was his tribute insufficient? Was Sennacherib unsatisfied, or did he change his mind? He sent his senior officers with an army to beat the city into surrender. Their tactics reveal that Assyrian warfare was not utterly brutal, the parley held out offers of escape from the terrors of military assault, promising a better lot (31, 32). Assyria had overcome many cities whose kings had rebelled (33–35), she had no reason to expect that Jerusalem would not fall to her. That Sennacherib sent a second message (19:10–13) may show he was too busy fighting on the Egyptian frontier to press the siege with full force.

Note: Sennacherib's own records specify Hezekiah's tribute and the capture of his cities, but do not claim the capture of Jerusalem. Sennacherib was murdered by his sons in 681 BC.

THOUGHT: How often is Assyria's lying claim made (18:25, end)? See Matthew 7:15; 1 John.

18;19 Hezekiah and Sennacherib (2)

Imagine yourself in Jerusalem. The Assyrian army controls every other town, and now the generals are outside the city with their troops around them. They are calling for the city to surrender. It's true what they say, Assyria is very strong. She has taken all the rest of Judah; perhaps the Lord has called her to capture Jerusalem, too. After all, Samaria fell to her. King Ahaz had been a loyal subject of Assyria and it was legally wrong for Hezekiah to rebel, so what they are saying could be right; perhaps Hezekiah is not to be trusted, he's a forlorn hope; maybe we'd be better off in the new homes the Assyrians promise. But can we trust the Assyrian promise of a peaceful life in a prosperous land even though they re-settled the people of Samaria in fertile places?

Assyria has won again and again. Will the Lord deliver us? Our leaders tell us to be silent, but they're not saying anything themselves. There has been a report that the prophet Isaiah brought an oracle to the king, but can we believe it? Apparently God promises that Sennacherib will go home and be killed there, without taking our city! Tell that to the Assyrians!

Now we've heard that the Rab-shakeh has relayed the message to his master and a letter has come back from the emperor: 'Give up, your God won't save you any more than the other gods saved their cities'. Yet the Lord did save us in the past. Hezekiah has gone to pray; he believes the oracle brought by Isaiah. He's right; our God is the only God, the others are not real. But will God show his power now?

Another oracle has been spoken by Isaiah: It was the Lord who let Assyria come this far, it is all part of his plan; he even controls Sennacherib! Assyria has gone too far, *she* will be the captive, dragged along on a rope. It's hard to believe that when her army is everywhere, but God will save us; let's wait, and trust him.

The news that came soon afterwards was unbelievable. The Assyrian army was decimated, Sennacherib went home to Nineveh and Hezekiah sent tribute to him there to ensure he did not return. It was not Judah's small forces, or the Egyptians whom Sennacherib had fought to a draw, who put him to flight, it was the angel of the Lord.

THOUGHT: Ephesians 6:10–18 reminds us of the Christian fight when we may find ourselves in the same position as Jerusalem, her king and her citizens. Let them encourage our faith.

18;19 Hezekiah and Sennacherib (3)

Sennacherib's messages to Hezekiah produced two answers from the prophet Isaiah, speaking in God's name. They deserve further thought.

The first (19:6,7) was a matter-of-fact forecast. The king was not to be afraid, for the Assyrian would go home without fighting him and there he would suffer the disgrace of assassination. The short, factual words stand in sharp contrast to the boasts of Sennacherib. He had conquered this place and that, captured their kings and gods, and would do the same to Jerusalem. Isaiah reported, 'Thus says the Lord', without any explanation. Sennacherib had belittled the God of Judah, whose claims did not need to be supported by his past record: he is; and what he says will happen *will* come to pass.

After Sennacherib's letter arrived and Hezekiah had prayed about it in the temple, Isaiah gave a longer reply (19:20–34). Hezekiah in his prayer had shown his knowledge of the truth hidden from Sennacherib. The Lord is the living God; it was therefore no surprise that Sennacherib had conquered other gods for there was no reality behind their wooden or stone statues, unlike the one 'enthroned above the cherubim'. But Assyria's military prowess was undeniable; if God were to save tiny Israel, his fame would spread. The answering oracle, a fine example of Isaiah's poetry, takes up Sennacherib's attitude and turns it back on him. He ridiculed Jerusalem, but she will laugh at him, she will remain inviolate, he will be forced by events beyond his control to go home (21,28). The boasts placed on the Assyrian's lips (23,24) echo the language of Assyrian inscriptions asserting the king's triumphs in exaggerated terms. Those inscriptions give the credit to the gods of Assyria; Isaiah's words reveal that God planned all. The purpose which lies behind the turning of cities into heaps of ruins is not revealed. We may suggest that it was in order to test the Assyrian and to make his fall greater, as another oracle implies (Isa. 10:5–19). Assyria led her captives home like animals with hooks and ropes (compare Amos 4:2), and that is how, in effect, the boastful king would return to Nineveh.

Judah suffered a terrible devastation, only the capital was saved and the land would take time to recover (29). What a story of God's deliverance the 'band of survivors' coming out of Zion would tell to cheer their war-torn countrymen. How had it happened? God's zeal, God's concern that man should not mock him with impunity, the need to show that he does answer the prayer of faith, would do this.

THOUGHT: Do I have Hezekiah's faith (15–19)?

Questions for further study and discussion on 2 Kings 12:17–19

1. Contrast the fortunes of Israel in relation to Damascus (13:1–7,25) with Judah's affair with Israel (14:11–14), and the characters of the kings of Israel and Judah at that time. How do you see God at work in these events?

2. Amos spoke to Israel under Jeroboam II. Read his prophecies beside 2 Kings 14:23–29. Did he have any effect?

3. What does the interaction of Ahaz with the Assyrians have to say to alliances between the church and the world, or the way that individual Christians should respond to the world's offer of various securities? Where should the line be drawn?

4. The refrain about the high places not being taken away (12:3; 14:4; 15:4,35) underlines the demand for complete loyalty and obedience that God placed upon his people at Sinai, extending through all parts of life. Identify modern 'high places' that distract from, or replace, the worship of the true God. How can they be destroyed?

5. With Samaria fallen, Jerusalem was left open to Assyrian attack; similarly, the fall of one Christian may expose another to harm. Find how Paul expected Christians to link arms in preventing this (eg. in Gal. 6; Col. 3; 1 Thess. 4,5).

20 Hezekiah's faith and Judah's fate

Hezekiah's illness occurred before Sennacherib's invasion (6) and Merodach-baladan's reign ended in 703 BC. After hearing his death sentence, Hezekiah prayed and wept. He felt God was rewarding him poorly for his loyalty. Was his illness a test of faith? Isaiah received a second, more positive, oracle. Now Hezekiah knew exactly how long a span of time was left to him and what would occur in that period. Despite his reforms, Jerusalem was to be saved only for the sake of David and of God's name (6). The medicine (7) was an ancient cure, prescribed outside the Bible for a sick horse! Hezekiah's demand for a sign recalls his father's rejection of an offered sign (Isa. 7; see also 19:29–31). Whatever the sign was (a shadow on the steps), it helped the king.

An embassy from a foreign king, notable as a rebel against Assyria, flattered Hezekiah. Its purpose may have been both congratulatory and conspiratorial, to raise the revolt in the west. Hezekiah's display would then have revealed his resources. Isaiah's rebuke points to the folly of relying on weapons and human help; in this Hezekiah was following Ahaz's bad example. The alliance so gladly entered, said the prophet, would give way to dominance by Babylon, and all the treasured stores would prove useless. Hezekiah's selfish reply (verse 19) may rest on a conviction that God would have mercy if his descendants proved faithful.

Note: *Hezekiah's conduit* is generally identified with the water tunnel leading from the Virgin's Fountain through the rock for 1750 feet (533 m.) to the Pool of Siloam.

THOUGHT: Consider Hezekiah's attitudes in ch. 19 in the light of 20:6. What differences would there be in your life if you knew in which year you would die?

21 Two evil kings

The exceedingly good Hezekiah sired Manasseh who became the most wicked king of Judah, according to the Hebrew writers, yet ruled longest of all. What Hezekiah had abolished, Manasseh replaced with interest. He was subject to Assyria, as cuneiform inscriptions and the longer account of his reign in 2 Chronicles 33 relate, but his religious activities did not stem from that, he was thoroughly reprobate himself. His pagan altars and images were not erected only in Jerusalem, but in the temple itself. He went down to the lowest depths, he was worse even than the Amorites whose evil had already brought their condemnation in the days of Abraham (Gen. 15:16).

Prophecy did not cease in Manasseh's day, although the names of the prophets are not known. Later traditions tell that it was he who had Isaiah sawn in two (compare Heb. 11:37). Extreme evil was matched with the severest punishment. The God of Israel had already dispossessed the northern tribes from the Promised Land; now Judah, only a remnant anyway, would be dispersed, too. Whatever penitence there might be would only postpone the execution. In that light, the author of Kings was not concerned about Manasseh's later repentance told by the Chronicler.

Manasseh's son continued his father's practices. His courtiers who killed him may have had a pretender of their own, but the citizens, loyal to the dynasty of David, rejected them and made the young Josiah king.

Note: Many commentators assume that the long reign of the wicked Manasseh embarrassed pious Jews, so they invented the idea of his repentance, given in 2 Chronicles 33, to account for it. Does the Old Testament in fact teach that the lives of evil men are regularly cut short?

THOUGHT: Had Hezekiah's reforms failed to fill the vacuum that abolition of pagan practices had left? Do churches feed their converts enough to replace worldly pursuits and thoughts (compare Luke 11:24–26)?

22 Josiah hears the word of God

The boy Josiah, like his great-grandfather Hezekiah, was brought up in the orthodox religion, despite his father's evil conduct. There were evidently two strands in upper levels of society, at least. One turned with the times, noisily embracing paganism under Manasseh's encouragement, leaving it as easily when he repented, doubtless happy to revert to it again under Amon. Another clung quietly to the true faith and was there ready to guide the new young king. By the age of twenty-five or so he was alert to the needs of God's temple. From 2 Chronicles 34 it is clear this was a stage in a royal reforming programme begun earlier. In the course of this a momentous discovery was made. The book of the law Hilkiah found in the temple had probably been lost by neglect or purposely concealed during the heretical years of Manasseh. Its identity remains in doubt but the majority of scholars believe it was Deuteronomy in view of the following reforms and the impact of the book on the king. The high priest had no doubt about what he had found (8), but the secretary introduced it to the king less specifically, so that its impact was greater (10).

As soon as the king heard the text, he was convicted. He knew there was a heavy penalty for disobedience, even though he had been unaware of these laws. His reaction is the more striking as he had already set out deliberately to reinstate the proper religion; he made no attempt to justify himself on those grounds. Though Josiah's apparently limited knowledge of God and his requirements had prompted the reforms, this book plainly showed that they were inadequate. He knew the questions God's word raised for him could only find satisfactory answers through God's spokesman, a prophetess.

Huldah's words warned and comforted. There was no way to escape the exile forecast in the book; the wrongdoing of one generation did affect the next and God's anger would run its course. Yet Josiah's desire for righteousness could not pass unmarked, the final catastrophe would not fall in his lifetime, as with Hezekiah (20:16–19). Here the role of the king in the nation is apparent. His personal initiative and his humility when his good deeds were shown to be unable to alter God's plan, in effect won the nation a short reprieve. The prophet Jeremiah, who had begun his work about five years earlier, uttered most of his oracles in that interval.

THOUGHT: Pray that you may read God's word as if you have only just discovered it.

23:1–27 Josiah acts upon God's word

Assured of God's mercy, Josiah took his stand in public, by the pillar (compare 11:14) to make his covenant (compare Deut. 17:14–20). His sincerity is noted, *with all his heart and all his soul* (3). The commands and warnings of the law were beyond doubt; the Lord alone would be worshipped in Judah. Every vestige of idolatry and syncretism was removed, however venerable (and the numerous items listed show how much there was).

To be effective, the purging had to be total. Worship of the sun and stars was widespread; they were held to represent divine beings, to influence men's lives and provide a means of telling the future. Being visible, they were easier to worship than the invisible God. Early Hebrew inscriptions found recently reveal that *Asherah* was treated as a consort of the Lord. The concept of a single Being of whom man and woman form the 'image' has always been hard to comprehend, so men have long provided a female partner for God, in various guises. In such situations the possibility of sexual licence can grow, and Josiah took steps to end the insidious lowering of morality that was encouraged. The catalogue of pagan practices abolished reveals the extent of the corruption among the people of God and within his temple. Josiah's reach extended across the political frontier into the Assyrian province of Samaria, to Bethel and beyond. Jeroboam's deceptive shrine was destroyed at last, desecrated beyond renewal by the bones burnt upon it (16,20; compare 14). By this time (*c.* 620 BC) Assyria's power was waning, so Josiah met no opposition in the northern territory.

The reform required the positive involvement of the citizens also. The great passover reminded them of how they came to be in the land, underlining the meaning of the covenant and the threats against its breach. All personal superstition had to go as well (24). Nevertheless, God's punishment was to come, God's name could not rest on a people that had so constantly rebuffed him. The reform seems to have had no lasting effect. The outward signs of paganism were removed, but their influence remained in hearts and minds that were not wholly repentant. The prophet Jeremiah continued to plead with his compatriots to return to the pure faith of Moses during the years that followed.

Note: *the man of God* (17), see 1 Kings 13.

THOUGHT: Was Josiah's reform 'too little too late' or an imposed rather than a voluntary and joyous conversion? Recall the covenant which enables you to be a Christian (John 17) and consider how you keep your part.

23:28–24:17 Judah in decline

In 612 BC the Assyrian empire collapsed with the fall of Nineveh to the Medes and the Babylonians. The last Assyrian king made a stand in north Syria, and Necho of Egypt hoped he could extend his power by an alliance with him. Josiah appeared to think this threatened his own independence. His rash intervention ended his reign and opened Judah once more to the rivalries of the great powers. Had he grown self-satisfied, or self-reliant, failing to meditate on God's law regularly, as Deuteronomy demanded? Earlier history showed how a foreign power was hard to oust once involved in the affairs of God's people. The danger has always been there and remains in the church. Josiah's son Jehoahaz, enthroned by the citizens, failed to follow his father's religious policies. His reign was cut short as Necho returned through Syria and installed his own nominee. The tribute and change of name displayed Egypt's ascendancy. Like his brother, Jehoiakim failed to put his faith fully in God.

In 605 BC Babylon defeated Egypt at the battle of Carchemish. The new king of Babylon, Nebuchadnezzar, forced Jehoiakim to become his vassal as part of his policy to secure his empire. When Jehoiakim rebelled, forces loyal to Babylon attacked Judah from all quarters until the army of Babylon could advance. During the siege of Jerusalem, Jehoiakim died, his son succeeding him only to surrender to Nebuchadnezzar (March 597 BC). Judah's punishment had begun. All the trappings of independence were removed, as were all the means of maintaining a prosperous society. Nebuchadnezzar set another son of Josiah on the throne as his vassal, calling him 'righteousness of the Lord' instead of his own name 'Gift of the Lord'. The foreigner's grip was tight.

THOUGHT: How do the events of these verses justify Zedekiah's name?

24:18–25:30 The end of the kingdom of Judah

Zedekiah's perversity, political and religious, is vividly illumined by Jeremiah 21–24,27. Inveigled by Egypt, Zedekiah broke his oath of loyalty to Babylon and rebelled, just as Hoshea of Samaria had done with Assyria (2 Kings 17). Nebuchadnezzar's punitive expedition was predictable. For six months Jerusalem withstood the siege. Archaeological excavations have uncovered the Babylonian arrowheads embedded in the city wall. Zedekiah's punishment was cruel, an example to others tempted to rebel. His supporters, priestly and secular, were executed. Jerusalem's fate was as bad, the temple was ruined and its equipment confiscated so that the worship of the God of Israel should no longer have a national basis. The citizens were deported, leaving the country on a subsistence footing. The poor remnant were left under the rule of a Jew loyal to Babylon who gave sound advice (25:24).

Astoundingly, some still thought the kingdom might be restored to David's family, and rose against the Babylonian's nominee. Seeing they could not win, they fled to Egypt, taking with them the prophet Jeremiah (for details see Jer. 40–44). So Judah's kingdom ended in exile and flight, as 24:20 explains.

The writer of Kings, like so many biblical authors, was sure God did not leave his people utterly hopeless. So he ended his work with a note of continuity. Jehoiachin's exile began in 597 BC. Babylonian documents record the issue of oil to him and his dependants in Babylon. In 562 BC Nebuchadnezzar died and his son favoured the imprisoned king. Ultimately, Jehoiachin's descendants would return to their land, led by Zerubbabel, and David's line would have some continuity until his 'greater Son' was born to usher in the age of the new Israel.

THOUGHT: Trace the number of good kings and the number of bad in Judah's history, and reflect upon God's mercy to his people, noting Genesis 18:23–32. How does this parallel your experience with God?

Questions for further study and discussion on 2 Kings **20–25**

1. Could the punishment of faithless Judah as a people be compared with the punishments threatened for churches in Ephesus and Pergamum in Revelation 2? If so, in what ways?

2. Find out which prophets spoke during the last forty years of Judah's life. Is it conceivable that their messages were totally ineffective?

3. Foreign nations were a major instrument of God's anger against his people, for they, too, were under his control (19:25,27,28). They could also be used for testing God's people. Compare Revelation 2:10,11, for a Christian 'translation'.

4. What sacrifices should be made to safeguard the heart of the gospel? Compare Hezekiah's attempt to preserve Jerusalem, 18:15,16.

5. Hezekiah destroyed the brazen serpent that had been an instrument of salvation but had become an object of worship (18:4). Are there objects, traditions, positions in your church which have been hallowed wrongly and need to be abolished because they prevent true worship?

Chronicles: Introduction

After reading Kings, Chronicles seems repetitious. Its opening genealogies lead to a history which is often identical with the books of Samuel and Kings, yet often parts company from them. In many cases a knowledge of those books is assumed, the writer not needing to repeat their narratives in order to make his point (compare the summary of Hezekiah's political history in 2 Chron. 32 with 2 Kings 18–20). Chronicles does have its own information, not found in other books. For a century it was fashionable for Old Testament scholars to treat this as the fabrication of the author, a means to convey his religious views. While such opinions are not extinct, many now agree that this distinctive material does rest on earlier records and has historical value of its own. Its presence is certainly connected with the purpose of the author, plainly one man (in contrast to Kings) who is known as the chronicler.

The chronicler was concerned to inculcate the right worship of God in his temple as prescribed in his law. God could only be worshipped by his true people, the real Israel, identified as David's tribe, Judah, and any others who sincerely obeyed the Law. (As a consequence of this the name 'Israel' is applied both to the whole nation and to Judah alone in Chronicles.) Everyone had his place and his task. When the temple services were properly performed, with music and song, God's worship was joyful and uplifting and his presence would be known to his people. The chronicler shared these views with the post-exilic prophets (see Hag. 1:7–11; Zech. 6:14,15; and Mal.) The continuity of God's people through many vicissitudes is displayed by the various generations which link the ancestors and famous men of the past to the chronicler's own time as one nation, the people of God.

The chronicler taught, too, that God is just, punishing the wicked and blessing those who trust him. These were particularly relevant doctrines for the returned exiles who no longer had a secular state of their own but centred their lives on the temple, united primarily by their religion (for many who were equally Jewish remained in their places of exile where they found a better livelihood). In this, Chronicles can speak to Christians today, a supra-national group, bound together only by common faith, a faith that needs to be traced to its foundations and followed through its history to be thoroughly understood, and which needs to be constantly reaffirmed, whatever the changes in circumstances.

Comparison of passages in Chronicles with the parallels in Genesis, Samuel and Kings reveals numerous small discrepancies. Some are clearly the products of scribal error, mis-spelling of names in lists being most common. The variations in numbers are greater. There may be errors (e.g. 2 Chron. 9:25: *4,000 stalls* is preferable to 1 Kings 4:26: *40,000*; 2 Sam. 8:4 to 1 Chron. 18:4; 1 Kings 7:26 to 2 Chron. 4:5). Other cases of larger numbers in Chronicles might be attributed to inflation (e.g.

1 Chron. 21:25 against 2 Sam. 24:24), or to unknown ways of calculating. Here it may be noted that some of the very large numbers in the Old Testament may be explained as the consequence of misunderstood terminology, the Hebrew words for 'captain' and 'one thousand' being similar. In this case the number killed in 1 Kings 20:27–29 becomes 100, not 100,000; and the 10,000 in 2 Chron. 25:12 becomes 10. (See J. W. Wenham in *The Lion Handbook of the Bible* (1973) p. 19lf; in detail in *Tyndale Bulletin* 18 (1967) pp. 19–53.)

Chronicles: Contents

1 Chronicles

1 The origins of Israel and her neighbours

These genealogical chapters are an important part of the books of Chronicles, however dull they may seem today. The first, drawing on Genesis chs. 5, 10 and 11, sets out the unbroken line of Israel's descent from the first man to Isaac and Jacob (note how the genealogy of Jesus in Luke 3 goes one step further back). This is not of vital significance in itself, for every nation could do the same, according to the biblical narrative. Rather, the value of the list lies in the lines which, besides Israel's, were traced from Noah. Some tribes and peoples were closely akin to Israel, some related only at a remote stage. Nevertheless, all were linked and therefore none could claim any inherent superiority to another in physical form, intelligence, or spiritual perception, even if their culture was as impressive as Egypt's. Herein lay one important reminder to Israel that her position as God's chosen people was not through special distinction of her own, but entirely through God's grace.

The groupings are clear (well displayed in the NIV), with certain geographical links. Problems in identification obscure the details in several cases and others are hard to explain in the light of modern knowledge (eg. the association of Caphtorim, the Cretans, with Egypt in 11,12). In this chapter and the following ones, *son* is not always to be understood as a precise term, it may cover more than one generation and, in the same way, *father of* may simply denote direct ancestry. The author has deliberately arranged these family trees so that all can be completed before he turns to Israel's own.

The rulers of Edom (43–54) were evidently tribal sheikhs in some sort of league whose cities may have been tented camps. The *chiefs* may have been war-leaders, the word *alluf*, their title, is used in modern Hebrew for 'Major-General'. The Edomites were of special interest to Israel for the ancient relationship of the two nations and their constant enmity. The fact that there were kings in Edom at an early date was presumably one of the reasons Israel demanded a king 'like all the nations' (1 Sam. 8:5). The temptation to be like others is always strong.

Comparison of the names in this chapter with those in Genesis exposes various minor differences resulting from scribal confusion (see NIV margin).

THOUGHT: Israel's world was more limited than ours. Even so, human beings are all related and all equal, whatever the boundaries and distinctions man may raise. There is one way the barriers can be overcome (see Gal. 3:27,28; Eph. 2:11–22).

2:1–4:23 The family of Judah

Chapters 2–8 present the family histories of the twelve tribes. Judah receives most attention because it included David's family (ch. 3). To follow the lines of descent the names should be set out in 'family tree' form, or a series of sub-headings used (as in NIV). Again, the lists are not in the precise step-by-step pattern of modern genealogists. Some generations are omitted (e.g. from Judah to David in 2:4, 9–15, is likely to have been longer than ten generations, say 300 years). The line of descent is what is maintained. Further, where a name is both a person's name and a place name, the intention was probably to say that the descendants of the 'father' occupied and named these places (e.g. many in 2:42–55, such as Kiriath-jearim, 2:50). In some cases men certainly gave their names to settlements they founded.

Chelubai (2:9) or Caleb (2:18,42) is to be distinguished from the non-Israelite Caleb, the famous colleague of Joshua (Josh. 14:6–15; 1 Chron. 4:14,15), although each had a daughter named Achsah.

The inclusion of historical notes such as that in 2:21–23 is a practice found in other ancient lists of ancestors and rulers. In this instance, the episode records a raid that probably occurred during the time of the judges. Later David married a daughter of the king of Geshur (3:2). These notes are also a reminder that the lists of names conceal real people who lived in the world and reacted with one another much as we do.

David's own family is given in considerable detail (3:1–9), his descendants limited to the ruling kings (3:10–16) until the time of the exile, again to show the line continuing. The author clearly had access to much more extensive information; compare, for example, 11:18–21 with ch. 21. With the exile the list grows again to embrace the whole family. Here, in a period of dispersion, a comprehensive record was needed to maintain and check family relationships, otherwise all sorts of impostors could have been troublesome. Anani (3:24), the last named of David's descendants, may have lived in the time of the chronicler.

THOUGHT: The inclusion of Achar ('Achan' of Josh. 7) displays integrity, for he could easily have been omitted. His inclusion stresses the solidarity of family and society; his action affected both his contemporaries and his children (cf. 1 Cor. 12:12–26).

4:24—6:81 Tribal genealogies

The descendants of Simeon settled in the very south of the promised land, as a mainly pastoral people. Although overshadowed by the more numerous and more powerful Judah (4:27), at one stage they were powerful enough to conquer part of Edom across the Arabah valley (the Meunites probably lived around modern Ma'an, east of Petra).

Reuben, Gad and the half-tribe of Manasseh (ch. 5) occupied parts of Transjordan. Their families are outlined, with notes of their lands. Separated by the river Jordan from their kin, their genealogies were collected at a moment of prosperity that gave leisure for such pursuits, under Jotham and Jeroboam II (5:17, compare 2 Kings 14:23–29; 15:32–36; 2 Chron. 27). Shortly after, Assyrian attacks broke up the clans by exile (5:6,26). One generation knew God's mercy 'because they trusted in him' (5:20). The two-and-a-half tribes together, by contrast, had a shameful reputation (5:25) and so experienced the full extent of God's justice (5:26).

Chapter 6 deals with the special tribe of Levi which supplied the nation with its priests and cultic personnel. Their names and duties are given with more detail in chs. 23–26. In verses 3–15 is a list of high priests down to the exile; once more it is an incomplete list, Jehoiada of 2 Kings 11 and 2 Chron. 22 being absent, with others. Another list in verses 49–53 covers the shorter span from Aaron to the time of Solomon, in connection with the organisation of the temple. There the musicians installed by David could trace their family lines back to Levi, too. (The sudden introduction of this reverse order would not disturb ancient readers so much as it may modern ones.) Levitical lands (54–81) were scattered throughout Israel to remind the tribes of their responsibilities. Moreover, when one course of Levites was serving in the temple, this arrangement ensured there would not be any extensive area of the countryside left under-manned.

Note: There are several textual difficulties, well shown in the NIV. Among them are the insertion of Samuel in 6:26, and the additional town names in 6:59,60 to agree with the total. Scribal errors are especially likely to arise in copying lists like these.

THOUGHT: Although set apart, God's ministers, the Levites, lived in the same way as their fellow-Israelites and among them. In what ways were they distinguished? Do they have any modern counterparts?

7:1–9:34 Tribes, king and people

Chapters 7 and 8 complete the tribal lists. The information in 7:2 can be applied to the figures in later verses and to 5:18. David's census (ch. 21) is a likely source. After Issachar comes Benjamin (6), yet ch. 8 is devoted to Benjamin. As the first son of each list (7:6 and 8:1) is Bela, yet the names of the subsequent ones differ, it is suggested a scribe wrote the wrong ancestral name in 7:6. The list in 8:1–3 agrees sufficiently with Numbers 26:38–40, whereas 7:6 does not. Instead of Benjamin, the list of 7:6–12 may have belonged to Zebulun, although these names are not the same as those in Numbers 26:26. Zebulun, however, is otherwise missing from 1 Chronicles 1–9 except for the Levitical part in 6:77. Dan is also absent, but 7:12 may conceal a Danite name in Hushim (Num. 26:42, Shuham). Dan, like the next tribe, Naphtali, was the son of Bilhah. Another confusion may underlie the name of Makir's wife and sister (15,16), but the identity could be coincidence.

Ephraim, Asher, and Benjamin are treated genealogically or by location. Various brief anecdotes serve to remind the reader that, despite any confusion in names, these were real human beings, who married and divorced (8:8), fought and died (7:21).

Benjamin's place is larger because of the special attention given to king Saul's family (8:29–40), although the writer did not name all the progeny of Ulam!

As a supplement, ch. 9 brings the information up-to-date, naming those who returned from exile in Babylonia. Here the chronicler exhibits his interest in the temple, devoting most of the space to the names and duties of the priests and Levites. Verses 1–16 have a counterpart in Nehemiah 11; the differences between them may arise from the use of lists compiled at separate times. The priests had the spiritual responsibility for the cult and services in the temple, the Levites were charged with the physical provisions and maintenance, ensuring that all was in order for the worship of God by his people. Every aspect of the services was to be carried out properly, both sacrifice and singing (9:33; compare 6:31,32). The failure of these Levites is described in Ezra 9,10; Nehemiah 13.

THOUGHT: Despite the problems in the details of these lists, they report to us the continuity of God's people over a thousand years. Each one, named or unnamed, had a part in the 'plan of salvation' to build the nation bearing God's name.

9:35–11:9 The king the people chose

Repeating the genealogy of 8:29–38 introduces Saul, but the chronicler was not concerned with his reign. The fact of his death and the end of his dynasty was what mattered to him, for without that, the theme of the next nineteen chapters, the reign of David, would appear in a vacuum. Further, there is a contrast between Saul dying by his own hand, defeated by the Philistines, and David, the famous warrior, victorious over the same enemy (ch. 14). Saul compares unfavourably with the Philistines in failing to give God his due (10:13,14), whereas they honoured their gods for their triumph (10:9,10). He knew he could not live with his failure, and the death of Jonathan ended any real hope he had of his line continuing. Notice the armour-bearer's fear of harming God's anointed king, even in his disgrace; compare David's restraint in 1 Samuel 24:6,10; 26:6–25. Should this attitude extend to all men created 'in the image and likeness of God'? Suicide is usually considered a usurpation of God's control of life; was Saul's argument sufficient justification? Had his earlier conduct brought him to this position? Although Saul died by his own hand, the historian can still say 'the Lord slew him'.

Whatever relief Saul had brought to Israel was cancelled by his unfaithfulness. The summary of 10:13,14 asserts the gravity of those actions. 10:1–12 repeats the 1 Samuel 31 narrative with slight variations that may indicate the author had access to a more complete record. Events attending David's accession are told in 2 Samuel, but they need not be repeated. The chronicler brings David to the throne at Hebron, then to the new capital, Jerusalem, so that he can move into an account of the king's glory and triumphs. The section ends with 11:9 to contrast David with Saul, 10:13. Observe how the latter's failure results from his acts, whereas his rival's rise was by God's will.

THOUGHT: The consequences of the leader's failure (10:7,13) remind us of the solidarity principle and its responsibilities; compare Romans 12:5.

11:10–12:22 David's heroes and followers

The chronicler has copied this list either from 2 Samuel 23:8–39, with slight variants, or from a common source, as far as verse 41. The glory of David's reign, which he is portraying, was not restricted to the king's prowess. David was the hub but he could not have achieved his kingdom without support from a wide variety of people and in those days the most notable were the warriors. These were not hired men, they were drawn to David by his personality. Although they were men of war, they had other attributes, too. Their loyalty was proved by their devotion to David. One can imagine them seizing the remark he made (11:17) without really meaning any action to be taken. David's reaction was a sign of penitence. Recognising he had jeopardised his men's lives, he offered to God what they had brought to him, for it is God who gives life and takes it.

How David's heroes were put in their order is unexplained. More great deeds are noted for Benaiah (11:22–25) than for any other in this list, although what his first was is still obscure (a king of Moab claims to have captured an *ariel*, according to the Moabite Stone). His second feat is a reminder of the threat that wild animals posed and of the extremes of climate in Palestine. The giant he killed was about seven and a half feet tall. Unbalanced diets and lack of medical control may have led to a higher incidence of gigantism in antiquity than is seen today. David and his men fought at least three of them. Yet, despite these exploits, Benaiah 'did not attain to the three'; Benaiah's character may not have been reliable, though his actions were brave deeds of the moment.

No doubt the rolls of honour in 11:26–47 and 12 gave pride to many later generations. While the majority of the names were Israelite, three foreigners also appear (11:39 Zelek; 41 Uriah; 46 Ithmah), for no one loyal to David was barred from his band, just as there was no bar on anyone loyal to the Lord joining Israel.

Notes: In 11:14 there is no need to replace the plural forms with singular; the text says David was fighting with Eleazar.

THOUGHT: How often do our words put others in spiritual danger (see Jas. 3:5)?

12:23–13:14 The ark

The men of Israel flocked to David in large numbers (the count is some 350,000, but refer back to Chronicles *Introduction*), enough to assure him of national support, which was reinforced by gifts of food from far and near.

At the centre of Israel's worship stood the ark of the covenant. Within it were the terms of the covenant which created Israel, engraved on tablets of stone. Upon it each year should be sprinkled the blood that atoned for Israel's failure to keep the terms of the covenant during the previous months (Lev. 16). During the upheavals of Saul's reign the ritual appears to have lapsed; the ark had lost its central place, though it was not forgotten. David, with the support of all the people, realised the ark should be in Jerusalem, at the heart of his kingdom. Its journey there was to be a triumphal event, carried out with proper regard to the sanctity of the symbol of God's presence (13:8), hence the summons to the priests and Levites.

The ark had stayed for twenty years where it stopped after the Philistines returned it. The journey through the hills to Jerusalem was short, but it was interrupted. As noted later, the mode of transport was not really correct (15:13), despite the respect shown by the provision of 'a new cart' (13:7). As the oxen stumbled, the driver acted instinctively (13:9). He forgot that only the priests could touch the ark, only the levitical family of Kohath could carry it (Num. 4:1–15). David thought Uzzah's punishment too harsh. Should he have known its history, how its human captors had suffered, how Israelites who had interfered with it had died (1 Sam. 6:19) because of its holiness? The reality of holiness was clearly seen. Applied to the physical world it reflected God's purity and righteousness. Uzzah, however highly he valued the honour of driving the cart, was not sanctified. Moreover, had he lived, the temptation to say, 'I saved the ark', would have been strong. If he had done so, the status of the symbol and of the One it represented would have been lowered to something within men's hands.

David's anger was predictable but unjustified. Evidently it was not God's will that the ark should enter Jerusalem just yet (compare 13:2). Was David's action prompted by pride as much as by piety?

THOUGHT: Do we go 'beyond our station' in trying to protect God's reputation? Are we angry with God or our fellows without really trying to understand them?

Questions for further study and discussion on 1 Chronicles 1–13

1. The genealogies at the beginning of 1 Chronicles remind us of the long history of Israel. Is there any value in tracing your own ancestry, or the generations of Christians since the first century? Do these family trees tell us anything about the purpose of life?

2. The genealogies were an inheritance highly valued but not preserved with complete accuracy. Does this circumstance pose any problems for the doctrine of the inspiration of scripture?

3. David's commission was to 'shepherd' Israel (11:2). Follow the role of the king as shepherd through the Old Testament and compare it with the duties of elders and pastors in the New Testament.

4. Consider 12:16–18. How do you react to new members who join your church? Do they find there the sort of qualities that drew these men to David and caused them to utter these inspired words?

14 David's success

Here David's kingship is confirmed in three different ways. His most powerful neighbour, Hiram, acts in friendship. Tyre was a state based on trade, that had grown out of the remnants of Canaan which Israel had not conquered (Josh. 18:3–7; 19:28,29). Its access to the forests of the Lebanon made it a source for the best timber for big buildings, cedar. Such an act as Hiram's was a mark of recognition and friendship, whatever bargaining may have been involved (compare 2 Chron. 2:13–15).

By taking more wives, David behaved as the people expected the king to, however wrongly (see Deut. 17:18), for the king's power enabled him to do almost as he pleased. His family history showed his folly.

David's long-standing enemies, although badly beaten, were not yet finally defeated. They set out to capture their enemy, while he was equally determined to rid himself of their threat. With Philistine forces free to attack, he could never rule securely. Here specifically he asked God's advice. Was he unsure of himself or of his troops, or was he sincere, acting as a leader of God's people should at all times? Defeat could bring on Israel worse oppression than they had known in previous years. God's answer was simple and clear, the victory was undoubted, the Philistine gods proved their uselessness, were taken and destroyed. Still unconvinced, the Philistines made another raid. This time God's commands were specific, the action would be his, David's part was to pursue and destroy. Note how close the enemy was to Jerusalem, Gibeon was only six miles to the north; even now the Philistines were not completely beaten (see ch. 18). David now controlled the important route up from the sea-coast to the capital. His reputation grew at home and abroad, enhanced by some recognition of divine favour.

Why ch. 14 interrupts the story of the ark in chs. 13 and 15 is not clear. 2 Samuel 5 and 6 show that the sequence of events was not as given here. Is there a pattern of spiritual reverses followed by successes in the narrative, i.e. ch. 13 followed by 14–16; ch. 17 by 18–20; ch. 21 by 22–29?

THOUGHT: What does this chapter teach about success and reputation as viewed by the world and by God?

15 The ark reaches Jerusalem

After the calamity of Uzzah (ch. 13), David took care to transport the ark in the way the law required. It was not his trophy but the symbol of the One who gave him victory. It was not the king of Israel who was carried into his capital in ceremonial procession with music and dancing; it was, in effect, Israel's God, the One who had called her into existence. With his detailed description the chronicler reminds his readers, exiles returned to a diminished and ark-less Jerusalem, of the solemnity and glory of the long-past occasion. While some might trace their ancestry back with pride to the men named here, they would also be called to their responsibilities in a less prosperous time. Was their attention to the knowledge of God's presence in Jerusalem as real, or were they like the returned exiles whom Haggai berated (Hag. 1)?

This time there was no stumbling, the Levites made their own thank-offering, no doubt conscious of Uzzah's fate. The number of animals suggests that this was a collective sacrifice for all the Levites.

The king threw himself into the celebration, not keeping apart or standing on his dignity, but dressed like others with a tunic ('robe') over his shirt ('ephod'). David danced to honour God, but his wife saw his energetic activity as an insult to herself and a demeaning of the king's person. She was unwilling to share and so sought to find fault. Michal has many brothers and sisters in the church still, for whole-hearted devotion and transparent sincerity always arouse suspicion among those who are 'respectable' but do not have such qualities.

Notes: *Alamoth, Sheminith* (20,21) refer to forms of music, the latter perhaps to an eight-stringed lyre or an eight note tone scheme.

THOUGHT: Structural, liturgical worship is alien to many Christians today, and can be deadening. Equally, a 'free-for-all' can be an obstacle to many. How does this chapter show what should guide the Christian in worship (compare 1 Cor. 14:26–33)?

16 The ark installed

David had prepared a new tent; the tabernacle and altar stayed at Gibeon (v. 39). Here the ark was welcomed. It had guided Israel through the desert and stood in the bed of the Jordan at the entry to the Promised Land. Now, as it came at last to rest in the capital, the promise of the covenant was fulfilled: God's people were in control of the land, they were a nation recognised by other nations and the name of their God was widely known. After its wanderings, the ark marked the place where God finally set his name.

All this is the theme of the hymn of vs. 8–22, the history of Israel from the time of Abraham. Here is the reason for Israel's praise and the substance of it, all 'the wonderful works' of the Lord. At the moment of success the people were called to observe its source and the process through which it had arrived. Looking back over their history, this occasion was one of stressing God's role. Holy, just and faithful, he was the Lord. Placed in the Psalter as Psalm 105, this poem of praise continues with some specific examples of the wonders which God wrought.

The second half of the hymn (vs. 23–33) provides a balance for the attention given to Israel in the first part. Her destiny was always to show the nature of God to her fellow men. Now, with David's kingdom secure, she could call on them to see what God had done for her. All could come to worship him, he is incomparable. All could see now what sort of God rules the world, who 'comes to judge the earth'. With slight differences, these verses re-appear as Psalm 96. The closing call to praise is a common line. Verses 35,36 recur in Psalm 106:47,48 and may belong to the time of the exile or later when many Israelites were scattered, away from their homeland. The chronicler may have brought existing hymns together to illustrate what he thought took place, but there is no good reason to suppose that at least verses 8–34 may not have been sung in David's day.

THOUGHT: How far does our praise centre on God and his doings, calling others to acknowledge him and join us? How could we improve it?

17 David's aim to build the temple

To the powerful king a tent seemed unworthy as his God's dwelling. David would build a permanent temple. It was not to be. Later David gave as the reason his life of warfare, for his bloodstained hands could not build the temple of the Lord of life (22:8). Was it also that David had his own ambition? Having built Israel into a respected power and set up a capital and erected a palace, he had done all that a great king should do, except to honour his God with a lavish temple. As David's idea rather than God's command it might glorify the king more, as 'David's Temple'. The response of verses 7–14 may suggest that.

Nathan's initial advice to the king was encouraging. Did he speak hastily, without God's direction? Certainly he had to withdraw next day! The evidence of God's blessing on David, 'God is with you', may have led him to agree to the king's proposal too readily, yet each move needed God's approval. That is stressed by the question in verse 6. Only at the time God chose should something so intimately related to him be done, and only in his way (the lesson of the ark).

God's words for David remind him of his career, showing whose doing all his success has been. David wanted to build God's house, but it is God who builds David's house. God's promise was that David should never be forgotten, a promise that still holds true.

In response David acknowledges, with proper humility, God's ruling of his life. Properly, too, he looks for the honour of God in his works (24). His words can be compared with Deuteronomy 7:6–8; 26:5–11, recalling the amazing way God brought Israel to nationhood. There is a parallel, too, for Christians, brought out in Ephesians 2:1–10. The promise of David's continuing kingdom and a son who should build God's house, can also be read in terms of the Old Testament and the New Testament. Solomon did the physical task, David's greater Son builds his new temple, see Ephesians 2:19–22.

THOUGHT: Psalm 127:1 is attributed to Solomon, but David came to understand it too. Whose house are you building, and why?

18 Military victories

Now the chronicler returns to David's success in war. The Philistines still presented a threat. In ch. 14 we read that they were driven back from the approaches to Jerusalem, now David takes the war into their own territory, capturing one of their five cities (Josh. 13:3), Gath, which probably controlled another route from the coastal plain where it entered the hills to go up to Jerusalem. Thus he contained the Philistines in the south-west of the land. Defeating Moab gave security to the tribes east of the Jordan, on their southern frontier.

It is not clear whether David attacked the Philistines, Moab and the king of Zobah, or whether they attacked him. The war against Hadadezer could have occurred after the events of chs. 19,20. Whatever the reason, the campaign north against Zobah, between the Lebanon mountains, leading to mid-Syria, was a major triumph. David seems to have attacked, perhaps unexpectedly, when Hadadezer was away from his base on a campaign to extend his own rule. One victory followed another, the real reason being God's support (6). Israel was now powerful and enriched, although not able to cope with very many horses. All this brought the friendly advance of the king of Hamath, relieved of an enemy without effort on his part. With conquered or friendly neighbours on almost every side, all could see that the Lord was with David (compare 6,13; 14:17).

Observe how domination of all these states did not lead to their incorporation into Israel. Garrisons were put into them and tribute exacted, but the people remained foreigners; only those who accepted her faith could become Israelites. The church, similarly, has brought suffering on herself by embracing men or ideas that are basically alien and by failing to keep them under control.

Ruling his own people was a heavy responsibility. David saw the task was done in the spirit of Deuteronomy 16:18–20. He delegated men he could trust to various duties, and his sons aided him.

Notes: 2 Samuel 8:1 names *Methegh-ammah* as the Philistine area conquered; this may be a term for the city and its villages, as Chronicles implies. *Shavsha* (16) may be a foreign name, *Seraiah* its Hebrew replacement (compare 2 Sam. 8:17). *Cherethites and Pelethites* (17) were the royal bodyguard (2 Sam. 15:18).

THOUGHT: Luke 16:9–13 makes an important distinction between friend and master; David kept the right perspectives. How do non-Christian friends and ideas affect you?

19;20 David and Ammon

David's good nature is evident in v. 2; the war with Ammon that followed was not of his seeking. He hoped to continue the good relations that Nahash had had with him. Nahash's son listened to his advisers rather than follow his father's example. They were wrongly suspicious of their newly powerful neighbour and anxious for their positions. So they insulted the Israelite envoys, thus insulting their king. (The shaving questioned their manhood, the nakedness their status, compare 2 Sam. 6:20.) The action was as good as a declaration of war. Ammon prepared, buying help from the north. It was not enough. Joab was too skilled a general to be trapped and he routed the two armies, but the Syrians invited another battle and David himself came to crush them.

Next year the Ammonite war was renewed, again with Joab in command of Israel's troops. After his brief comment about David (20:1) the chronicler leaps over the disgraceful story of Bathsheba (2 Sam: 11,12) to the final triumph over Ammon. David's gross sin was not within the scope of the chronicler's narrative and could be read in Samuel. When the capital, Rabbah, or Rabbath-Ammon (modern Amman) fell, David took the triumph (compare 2 Sam. 12:27–29). The subjugation of Ammon was complete and the Hebrew text states there was a cruel massacre (compare AV, RV, RSV mg), but most commentators agree that the text of 20:3 should be altered, as in RSV, to indicate hard labour.

For the Philistines, giants were evidently a recognised military advantage. The phenomenon may have been the result of a genetic defect in a particular clan. Nevertheless, Israel had men to overcome them. David had shown the way!

Notes: The crown (20:2) may have been on the statue of the Ammonite god, Milcom, rather than on the local king (*Milcom* is almost identical with '*their king*' in Hebrew). By taking it David asserted his superiority. Its weight, about 30 kg, made any 'wearing' by a man symbolic. For the problems in reconciling 20:4–8 with 2 Samuel 21:19 see D. F. Payne, *New Bible Commentary Revised* pp. 318f.

THOUGHT: Was Joab's 'may the Lord do what seems good to him' fatalism, or real faith that God would fight for his people, a conviction that they were in the right? Where is our faith as we face unjust attacks?

21:1–22:1 David harms his people

Even the greatest God-given prosperity presents possibilities for sin. David, at the height of his power, wanted to know how strong he was; but this seems a natural and understandable ambition, something other kings would, and did, do. The chronicler passed over David's personal sin with Bathsheba, but reported this failure as fully as the writer of Samuel. Obviously one consequence was important to him, the purchase of the temple site. Yet more than that was involved. David had many victories, but time and again he faced armies larger than his own. David won not by numerical strength, nor by his own strategy, but only because *God* gave his enemies into his hands (eg. 14:8–17). As at Jericho (Josh. 5:13,14) other forces fought with God's people.

David evidently fell prey to pride, perhaps he dreamt of using his forces for further conquests, perhaps he wanted to compare his initial position with his present one (12:23–37); commentators mention Jeremiah 17:5–10 here. Joab, whose career was marked by concern for David's supremacy, objected to the king's plan. His point was that David could rely on his people, and the Lord would ensure they were adequate (3). David over-rode the objection, so Joab did what the king commanded but incompletely, for he knew the result would be disaster.

2 Samuel 24:1 depicts David's sin as the result of God's anger, here 'Satan incited David'. Job 1,2 may throw light on these attitudes.

Realising his sin, David chose the quickest punishment from the hand he knew, and God's experienced mercy was seen again (15). Yet David's action cost 70,000 lives, innocent, he realised, of the offence. David's guilt is affirmed and God's control of life and death is asserted.

David's sacrifices were accepted (26,27) although he was not assured of forgiveness (30). It was right that the threshing floor which he bought as a sign of penitence should be the site of Israel's worship for a thousand years, a place where the king acknowledged his fault.

Note: The different prices in 2 Samuel 24:24 and v. 25 may cover different areas of ground. The numbers mentioned here are larger than those in 2 Samuel 24:9, probably because they include the army (cf. ch. 27).

THOUGHT: God did not do as David suggested (17). Does the continuing history of David's family explain why (see, eventually, Matt. 1:1)?

Questions for further study and discussion on 1 Chronicles 14–22:1

1. Examine the content of your favourite Christian songs and hymns. How many both praise God and instruct the singers in the way 16:8–34 does?

2. David gave the 'silver and gold' he had carried off from the nations (18:11) to God. What share of the good things you receive do you give to God? (Compare the action of Abraham, Gen. 14:20; and 2 Cor. 9.)

3. What lessons do David's relations with foreign powers teach the church for its relations with secular powers and groups today?

4. David's census seems to have stemmed from natural pride (21). How can Christians guard against similar sins when they are given material success? Note 2 Corinthians 11,12; 1 Corinthians 2:14–16.

5. Do the deaths in 21:14 suggest that God used those people as pawns, suddenly depriving them of life to impress on David the enormity of his sin? Compare the fate of Job's dependents (Job 1:17–19) and the people in Luke 13:1–5. Is there a satisfactory answer, or should the Christian take refuge in Abraham's faith (Gen. 18:25b)?

22:2–19 Supplies for temple-building

The temple of the Lord, God of Israel, creator of heaven and earth, was to be no third-rate chapel made of whatever was to hand. For all his failures, David really trusted God and knew him as the only God (16:8–36; compare Ps. 8). Therefore the temple should be as glorious as human skill could make it (5). The preparations evidently continued over some years, beginning before the king succumbed to old age (1 Kings 1). In observing the detail of the materials, we should remember that they were all hand-worked. Most of this labour was laid on non-Israelite residents.

The charge to Solomon repeats parts of 17:11–14 and is taken up in ch. 28. It deals with two aspects of the supplies. The materials were so enormous in amount (14–16), over 3,700 tons of gold and ten times that in silver, that only divine providence can explain them, or simple hyperbole (by contrast with the amounts in Kings, see on 1 Kings 9,10). Some requirements could be met in the course of construction, most should be ready beforehand (compare Luke 14:28–30). More vital were the spiritual aspects. The builder could not be one who achieved his power by bloodshed lest the temple become a monument to war. Rather, the builder should be called 'Peaceful', Solomon, for the God of Israel is the God of Peace. Solomon inherited the promises made to David, but he had to work to see them fulfilled. God might be with him, but he had to 'keep the law . . . observe the statutes' all the time. The call to 'fear not' (13), echoing Joshua 1, came from one who had proved what he advised. The people were exhorted, too; God had used David to bring the peace they enjoyed, they should have one aim and set to work. King, people, alien residents – all were involved in some way. Today the building is known as 'Solomon's temple', but when it was planned it was to be 'a house for the name of the Lord'.

THOUGHT: How much care do we take to ensure we are qualified to carry out a work for God? What standards do we set for the work and what is our real aim (5,12,19; compare with 1 Cor. 3:11–15)?

23;24 Preparations for temple service (1)

As for the entry of the ark (ch. 15), so for the temple. All the personnel had their duties allocated. It was essential for the many Levitical families to know their places if there was to be order. Assigning positions by lot avoided any favouritism and the record prevented disputes (24:5,6,31).

Israel's temple was for the worship of the holy God, so there was to be no haphazard, casual entry as anyone pleased, and no cause for an individual to step out of line. This was the centre of the nation's faith which all the world would watch. Rivalry and feuding over privileges would be disgraceful (24:2, compare Num. 16). The priests were the most senior division of Levites (24:1–19; compare 23:13). Their honourable rank brought strict limits on their conduct and social life (Lev. 21). The large numbers of Levites meant that full-time attendance was required of only a few, most would farm at home until their fortnight's turn of duty or a major festival came. While in Jerusalem they were fed from the offerings brought to the temple.

Now the ark and tabernacle had a permanent home. So the function of those charged with carrying and erecting the portable shrine would change. This did not mean redundancy, only adjustment. A fixed building would need more cleaning than a movable tent. Sweeping the temple courts might seem a lowly task, but to counter the drudgery was the privilege of praise (23:30). In the wilderness the Levites began to serve at thirty; reducing the age meant a larger supply, so each was absent from home less often, thus able to support his family properly. The whole affair was supervised by the king, intent on honouring God with the most efficient service man could provide.

Note: Zechariah, John the Baptist's father, belonged to the eighth group of Aaron's descendants (Luke 1:5,8,9; compare 1 Chron. 24:10). The pattern set out here continued to the end of the Jerusalem temple, and devout Jews still traced their positions in it long after that.

THOUGHT: 'A servant with this clause
Makes drudgery divine;
Who sweeps a room, as for Thy laws,
Makes that and the action fine.'   (George Herbert)

25;26 Preparations for temple service (2)

Music had a vital role in Israel's worship. Essentially this was a corporate activity, uniting the worshippers. Nevertheless, leaders and order were necessary, so these Levites were divided into groups. Here were the musicians with percussion and stringed instruments, and the people would sing in praise to God to their tunes. In the headings of Psalms 39,62,77 *to* or *according to Jeduthun* appears to denote the style of music or tune. Asaph, however, composed several psalms, or they were written in his honour (Psalms 50,73–83); others of these musical men may also have contributed to the Psalter. Indeed, composing psalms or hymns can well be included under the term 'prophecy' (25:1–3), for it is a form of speaking on behalf of God words that men can use for themselves. Inspiration for those tasks came from God and impetus from the king, another tribute to David's own skills with words and instruments. Notice the equality ruling in this service for God, which rested on the gifts he had given (25:8).

For the temple to function there had to be a police force, the *gate-keepers* of 26:1–19, mentioned in 9:17–27. They had to open and shut the gates at the right times, ensuring that no-one was within the precincts who should not be and, no doubt, they kept out stray animals and anything that might defile the holy place. Acts 21:30 and Matthew 27:65 show them in action. Again, the places were taken by lot, no-one could claim his harder post was the result of personal feeling.

The *treasurers* (26:20–28) bore the same responsibility as their modern counterparts, with a special group to look after the erratic income from spontaneous giving (26:26–28), as opposed to the regular tithes and offerings. The *officers* and *judges* (26:29–32) seem to have been assessors and collectors of taxes and tithes, showing how closely temple and state were associated in the economy of God's people.

Note: The *Heman* of Psalm 88 was probably the Judahite of 1 Chronicles 2:6, not the Levite named in 25:6. In 25:8 *teacher* is better rendered 'skilful' as in v. 7, or 'experienced'.

THOUGHT: Many men are honoured by the record of their names in these chapters. The unnamed were as essential and all were equal. Each served God in the place he was given, illustrating Paul's figure of the body (1 Cor. 12:12–26).

27 Arrangements for running the state

A monthly rota of 24,000 men was organised to maintain the king's military and policing strength (1–15). In the main they would have served as garrisons throughout the realm, as escorts and as police, but any other jobs not held by specific officers could have fallen to them, especially to those stationed in the capital. The rota enabled men to know in advance when their turn would come and be able to make domestic arrangements accordingly. They were not called up at the king's whim as seems to have happened in some states. Some of the commanders have already appeared in ch. 11.

Tribal loyalties survived the organisation of the kingdom and each had a leader to represent their interests. Why Aaron figures in the list as well as Levi, but not Gad or Asher, is unknown. Some fault may have occurred in transmission. What is clear is that every Israelite had a means of access to justice, to the king. For the census and the incomplete number see 21:5.

Samuel had forecast the demands a king would make on Israel (1 Sam. 8:11–17) and 25–31 reveal this in effect. David's interests entered every aspect of the country's farming, here summarising its main branches. David could rely on these to meet the needs of his court; his son required more (1 Kings 4). Some of the estates may have been Saul's, some came to David through marriage (or with Abigail, 1 Sam. 25), some may have been purchases. Their royal ownership meant there was less land available for individual Israelites, even if the king provided employment.

Finally, 32–34 list David's counsellors. Joab and Jehoiada son of Benaiah (or Benaiah son of Jehoiada, 5) held offices named in 18:15–17. These men were experienced, talented (the Absalom story exemplifies this, 2 Sam. 15–19) and totally committed to David; counsellors he could trust in all situations. Hushai's title, *king's friend* (borne also by Zabud, 1 Kings 4:5, under Solomon), may denote a special intimacy that allowed him to stand in for the king.

THOUGHT: The position of a friend is a special one; contrast David's friend and his counsellors with Job's. How does your friendship to others and to your King measure up to John 15:13–17?

28;29 Provisions for the temple and its builder

Solomon's enthronement was the formal confirmation of the hurried process described in 1 Kings 1:39 (compare 1 Chron. 29:22). The assembly comprised the leading men listed in chs. 23–27, as representatives of the nation. The day before this ceremony, David gathered these men and set out his hopes to them, as he had previously to Solomon (22:6–16). Again he asserted God's elective grace, his choice of Solomon, and his decision that the temple be built (28:4–6). The conditions of Solomon's rule are repeated, 'if he continues . . .' (28:7). While humanly David's son, the new king was designated God's son to demonstrate the relationship the leader of God's people had to God. The formula of v. 6b (and 22:10) is taken up in Psalm 2 which explains something of the promise involved. Follow this thought further, as developed in the person of David's 'greater Son', in Colossians 1 and Hebrews 1, for example.

Solomon's task was prescribed in detail. David gave plans that he received from God, possibly the designs of the tabernacle (Exod. 25ff) modified for a permanent building of wood and stone. All the resources were collected and the people were prepared. To start the work one more ingredient had to be added: Solomon's whole-hearted devotion and zeal. If *he* did not start and finish the building it might never be completed, bringing dishonour to the Lord.

The cost would be tremendous. David made the most magnificent gifts from his own resources (29:3–5) and with this example could call on others to follow. The result brought joy to all. The temple would be no private 'chapel royal', but truly the nation's holy place. David's prayer is a high point in Old Testament expressions of faith, one that can be repeated by every devoted servant of God today. Devotion, praise and sacrifice belong together in any real worship. Sincerely and correctly offered (29:17) they bring assurance of God's acceptance, and so gladness (29:21,22, compare Exod. 24:11; Deut. 27:7).

David's work was done; Solomon was hailed and accepted by men (29:24) and God (29:25). The great king died. The chronicler knew he could say much more that went beyond his purpose, so referred interested readers to other works, now lost.

Note: *daric* (29:7) was a Persian unit of currency weighing little less than a shekel, current in the chronicler's time.

THOUGHT: How far does 28:9b apply to Christians today? Compare 29:17.

Questions for further study and discussion on 1 Chronicles 22:2–29:30

1. The temple arrangements (23–26) may appear regimented. How far was this necessary for a national shrine? Was it purely practical, or does it reflect an aspect of God's nature? How far should such organisation characterise a Christian church (compare 1 Cor. 12–14)?

2. David planned the temple as a resting-place for God's footstool (28:2). What does this say about David's conception of God (see, too, the following verses)?

3. God's footstool was the ark. Trace the early history of the ark and discover its purpose. It was vital to Israel's faith; how was it the place where God and his people could meet?

4. Do such expressions of dependence as 1 Chronicles 29:11,12,14–16 imply there is no place for human effort? Explore the concept 'man plants, man waters, but God gives the increase', noting 1 Corinthians 3:7.

2 Chronicles

1;2 Solomon's greatness

David's arrangements enabled Solomon to begin his reign with the major building project. Even so, the new king was called to take a step himself, to show his faith that God could give him whatever he asked. What follows has the theme of 'greatness'. Solomon's great splendour and reputation were given him by God (1:1). The people he ruled were great in terms of numbers because God had protected them (1:10). The temple would be great, too, because the God it served is the greatest of all 'gods' (2:5). To illustrate Solomon's riches, 1:14–17 tell of his chariotry and horses, costly and prestigious items, precious metals and timber. Huram of Tyre's friendly welcome for the new king's approach illustrates the 'honour' promised to Solomon (1:12).

The messages of Solomon and Huram are more elaborate here than the versions in 1 Kings 5. In neither case are they necessarily to be understood as complete transcripts, but as abridgements. The chronicler, with his particular religious interests, included more than the compilers of Kings. Solomon's expressions of devotion in the purpose he stated may seem excessive for a diplomatic letter, yet ancient writers delighted to spell out such details and to affirm their religious zeal. Solomon did not hesitate, either, to assert the superiority of Israel's God (2:5). So long as he realised there was no place for any other, he prospered (compare 1 Kings 11). In his reply, Huram assured his brother king of continuing good relations, of his readiness to supply what Solomon needed at the price offered and added his praise to God. His phrase that Solomon ruled because 'the Lord loves his people', is significant. Wisdom, knowledge and devotion to God were qualities Huram believed Solomon had, and they were given for the good of his subjects; he was not a tyrant.

There was no objection to importing foreign craftsmen to take charge of the decoration of the temple (although Huramabi was Israelite on his mother's side). Solomon wanted the very best for God's house, wherever he could find it. Earlier, Israel had employed the services of Bezalel, a craftsman from the tribe of Judah (Exod. 31:2–5).

Notes: *Huram* is simply a variant of *Hiram*. 2:2 may be a mistaken repetition of 2:18. For the amounts mentioned in 2:10, see *IBD* or *NBD* or NIV margin.

THOUGHT: Solomon used the opportunity of a normal diplomatic letter as a means to assert the uniqueness of his God. How can we use our normal activities in the same way?

3;4 The temple built

The chronicler abridges the description of the temple and its furnishings given in 1 Kings. Reading it, we should remember that it was written for people who had not seen the building, but knew Zerubbabel's temple. The plan was simple: one passed through the porch into the nave, which led on into the holy place. The high priest was the only person to enter this, and then only once a year. The two rooms were entirely gold inside. A multi-coloured curtain, the veil, separated the nave from the holy place, probably hanging in front of the doorway specified in 1 Kings 6:31,32. All the equipment within the building was also of gold (4:19–22). Items standing outside were of bronze, weather resistant and less obvious to thieves.

The holy place was the home of God. While thinking Israelites knew he was not limited to a single earthly shrine, this was the focus of their worship. Here alone could they offer sacrifices to him, so only here could they be sure he accepted them. The nation was created to be God's people. Its unity and life depended upon its faith more than anything else, so that faith needed a visible, physical centre. When the people's faith was not their primary concern, they split into factions, a tendency which always hampered God's purpose for his people.

The great quantities of gold were not ostentatious. Gold was appropriate for the house of God because it was the most costly decoration man could provide and because its unchanging, uncorroding nature made it the best picture of the purity attached to the eternal God. When the numbers of daily sacrifices, priests, and the regulations to ensure the holiness of all that was done are remembered, the need for pots, tongs, snuffers and all the other equipment becomes intelligible. Now, although the veil is torn away, the demand for holiness is just as strong (see Heb. 10).

Note: The height (3:4) seems excessive, and may be an error for thirty cubits (1 Kings 6:2). *Parvaim* (3:6) was either the name of the place of origin of the gold, or a designation of its quality. *Mount Moriah* (3:1) is the first identification of the temple site with the place where Abraham offered Isaac (Gen. 22:2).

THOUGHT: God's people are no longer a localised nation, yet a common centre is still essential for their unity. Church history repeatedly demonstrates what happens if that centre is not Christ. What is his place in your church?

5 The temple occupied

The last thing to be brought to the temple was the symbol of God's presence, the ark. The lessons of David's reign (1 Chron. 13–15) were learnt: all was done with great care, the Levites carrying the ark from its lodging in Zion to the new home a little to the north, the priests taking it into the sanctuary. This was no small matter, nor was it a royal ceremony, representatives of the whole nation were involved. Within the ark the tablets contained the covenant, the charter of Israel's existence, the promises and commands, the blessings and curses God had uttered through Moses long before. As the ark entered, innumerable sacrifices proclaimed the devotion of king and people. *The feast which is in the seventh month* was probably the feast of tabernacles, a week of thanksgiving and offerings, beginning a few days after the day of atonement (compare Lev. 23:26–36; Deut. 16:9–15 and 2 Chron. 7:9–10). The timing was appropriate, God came to dwell with his people (13) after the atonement was made, at the moment when their harvest reminded them that even their land was his gift. There was no notion of 'secular' as opposed to 'sacred' in those days, faith and daily life went hand in hand, each contributing to the other.

The cherubim overshadowing the ark were imaginary creatures, perhaps based on the sphinxes and griffons of Egypt, which symbolised another world and supernatural power. They stood, in effect, both to guard the sacred box and to act at God's command. No-one saw them except the high priest, so they remained mysterious, adding to the awe of the holy place.

Solomon's celebration brought all the clergy together, and they sang of the Lord's goodness, his daily provision for them and their consequent safety. Israel discovered that her God was reliable, just and merciful. The arrival of the ark in the temple marked the climax of his promises, God dwelt among his people in the land he had given them.

Note: *to this day* (9) is already present in 1 Kings 8:8 and represents the old text taken over by the chronicler without up-dating.

THOUGHT: Praise the Lord in the words of v. 13, recounting your experiences of his goodness and steadfast love.

6 Solomon's prayer of dedication

The great work completed, Solomon consecrated it and the whole nation to God. His first words appear to be a brief address to God (1,2). He then reminded the people of the events that had led to the present situation. The emphasis is strongly on God's part. He fulfilled his promise, he chose Jerusalem, he chose David, he allowed Solomon to build. In each case the co-operation of human agents was essential: David did not become king without effort, nor did the gates of Jerusalem open miraculously as his men approached. What Solomon had done was done 'for the name of the Lord'.

God's past goodness gave an assurance for the present and for the future. Solomon called on God to continue his faithfulness to David's family, as promised. Then he turned to the relationship between God and the people. God's greatness is awe-inspiring, yet the king was convinced that he would take notice of Israel and her prayers and that his nature was forgiving. In the light of this, Solomon could continue to pray for God to show his mercy when the people sinned. The examples begin at the level of man against man, then go on to concentrate upon offences against God. Defeat, drought and being overrun by pests were all seen as means of divine punishment. This may not always be the case today, but Solomon knew that where God's people were concerned everything had purpose and plan.

One of the most explicit statements of Israel's missionary purpose, and the door God held open through her to all the world, appears in 32,33. The foreigner was not drawn by Israel, or to her, but to the Lord whom he had seen act on Israel's behalf.

Foreigners could be hostile – 24,34,35. Solomon saw battle against them as a 'holy war', directed by God to achieve his purposes for Israel. Too often men have fought in God's name, with their own interests paramount.

The wisdom Solomon requested appears throughout his prayer, especially in 36–39. Throughout the prayer, too, sin and punishment, penitence, prayer, forgiveness and restoration, recur. The sequence is clear, but not automatic; the penitence has to be real (38).

THOUGHT: Solomon was awed that God would dwell with man on earth (18), yet he saw only the bright cloud which declared God's presence. With what degree of awe do we realise that he did dwell with men on earth, and that the Holy Spirit does still?

7 Solomon's feast of dedication

It is difficult to reconstruct the order of events in the great celebration. The fire from heaven consumed the sacrifices described in 4–7, or at least the first of them, for v. 4 opens with a clause that is best rendered in a simultaneous sense, rather than sequentially. The holocaust that Solomon offered was not mere show (the number of sheep was slightly more than the annual tribute Ahab received from Moab, 2 Kings 3:4), it had to be a recognisable proportion of his wealth to encourage the people. Some of the sacrifices were completely burnt, some provided meat for the worshippers. With God's presence evident, the people rejoiced. Eating and drinking in the presence of God only followed acknowledgement of sin and penitence, and God's acceptance of the sacrifice at the altar (compare Deut. 12).

With the celebrations over and the great day past, a sense of anti-climax can easily set in. At such a moment one can be caught off-guard. But it was at that moment that the Lord spoke again to Solomon (12–22). His words concern the whole nation first, taking up the major part of Solomon's prayer. Their faithfulness is directly related to their prosperity. Disasters are to be understood as divine discipline – sharp but, if effective, followed by forgiveness and blessing. As the agricultural community needed the right conditions all through the year, so God required sustained, continuous faith. Emphasis was laid on the one place of worship to encourage national unity and to discourage local cults that could become idolatrous. Then the address turns directly to the king. God's promise is clear. Equally clear is the threat which embraced king and people, for they could not be separated. Again, Israel's witness to the nations is shown to be important because it was to be through this that others would realise God was at work. Thus the celebrations closed with a sombre warning, repeating the warnings of earlier chapters. The splendid temple stood conditionally; it could tumble at any time. Its fate was in the hands of the people and their leaders.

THOUGHT: How firmly founded is your church? Does Israel's career have anything to teach it? Is the threat of Revelation 2:4,5, relevant to it?

8;9 Solomon's power and glory

Here the chronicler reports how God's promise at the king's accession (1:12) was fulfilled. That promise was not conditional on Solomon's continued faithfulness, it was God's reply to his request for wisdom.

Firstly he tells of an unexpected bonus. The cities of 8:2 were apparently those Huram had scorned when Solomon offered them as payment for his services (1 Kings 9:10–14). Thus a part of the Promised Land was retained.

Secondly, other imperial matters follow. Garrison posts and revenue centres were essential to sustain the wide-spreading state; Hamath-zobah lay well to the north, and Tadmor, later Palmyra, far to the north-east.

Thirdly, enslaving the remnants of the Canaanites provided a convenient work-force for construction projects. This slavery was nothing like the massed bands of Roman or more recent dictators, but a liability to be put to work whenever demanded, in the manner of the press-gang. Israel should have eradicated these people and, although they were useful, they remained a source of pagan influence. The marriage to Pharaoh's daughter increased that pagan influence, and her presence clearly raised some scruples in Solomon's conscience (8:11).

Fourthly, Solomon's religious practices are presented in more detail than in 1 Kings 9:25. It was important that the king should be seen taking the lead in the nation's worship, ensuring its proper support. Only with such regular worship could Solomon's 'work' be said to be done.

The fifth way God's promise was fulfilled was in successful trading ventures (8:17,18; for *Ophir* see comments on 1 Kings 9:28). These five items are balanced by 9:13–28 which recount Solomon's wealth and imperial glory. Between, comes the famous Queen of Sheba story, repeated from 1 Kings 10. Her verdict on Solomon is well-known (9:6); her praise was for Solomon's God.

Finally, the author refers to other sources. No doubt they told of Solomon's decline, as in 1 Kings 11, but their presence here would have upset the chronicler's aim to tell of God's faithfulness to Solomon.

THOUGHT: It is not the beginning that is effective in a church's witness, but the daily maintenance of its service. Solomon drew on what God gave him to establish the temple; the people provided continuing support.

10:1–11:12 Rehoboam's folly

Solomon's son did not ask God for wisdom as he began to reign, instead, he sought only human advice. The result was disastrous. His opponent, Jeroboam, had opposed some of Solomon's actions and received God's promise of kingship (1 Kings 11:26–40). His return from exile did not signal immediate revolt. He seems to have led a party seeking lighter taxes. Notice that his petition was accompanied by a promise of loyalty (10:4) although the book of Kings reveals that the kingdom had been promised to him earlier. Was it just perversity that inspired Rehoboam's arrogant answer? The chronicler sees it as God's work, but we may still ask what was in the king's mind. A determination to outshine his father, to be able to say, 'I have done this', may be suspected. So he played into Jeroboam's hands. The unity of the twelve tribes was always hard to maintain unless all were threatened by an external enemy. A strong or admired leader like Moses or David could command universal affection; Rehoboam could not. Even when the revolt was declared he tried to impose his will, first causing the death of his taskmaster, then planning the deaths of many more. His intended war was aborted through God's oracle given to the people, an interesting case of divine provocation to civil disobedience because the king had spurned God's way.

Frustrated and impoverished, Rehoboam set about strengthening his little kingdom. Israel was a potential enemy in the north and her new king had an ally to the south-west of Judah, the king of Egypt. Common sense required some attempt at self-defence, in contrast to the foolish thought of forcing Israel to surrender.

There could hardly be a greater difference than that between the characters of Solomon and Rehoboam. They had one common feature: each was given the opportunity to enjoy the fulfilment of God's goodness, and each forfeited it.

THOUGHT: The faithfulness of God – Rehoboam held his throne only because of God's promise to his grandfather David. How much do you, your church and your country enjoy because of your fathers' faith and God's faithfulness to them?

11:13–**12**:16 Rehoboam's reign

The division of the kingdom led to religious tension for those faithful to God in Israel. When Jeroboam set up his independent shrines at Bethel and Dan, the staff of the Jerusalem temple could not continue to live in the northern kingdom. Their removal meant the loss of their ancestral land-holdings, bringing an extra burden to Judah, and the loss to the Israelites of teachers and priests of the orthodox faith living among them. The temple revenues will have been greatly reduced at the same time as this new burden fell on Judah, even though some of the faithful still came on pilgrimages from the north.

Rehoboam apparently dealt with his large household more sensibly than with his kingdom, earning a word of approval (11:23). In taking so many wives and concubines, he was following the pattern of his father and grandfather, a pattern which is not condemned in its ancient context, but which subsequent events often showed to be full of danger.

What the apostasy of Rehoboam and Judah was, passes unexplained; most likely they turned to the pagan cults Solomon had permitted to gain a foothold in the land (see 1 Kings 11:33). In punishment, Shishak was brought to attack. His own inscription, on a temple wall in Karnak, lists scores of towns captured in Palestine, not including Jerusalem, but the list is incomplete. The capital was despoiled of its treasures but not sacked or occupied by the Egyptians; this was God's first warning. Judah's repentance mitigated the punishment. Gold replaced by bronze (12:10) symbolised the decline experienced in every aspect of national life. Life continued but at a lower level.

Note: *high places, satyrs, calves* (11:15) – the chronicler paints Jeroboam as black as possible to emphasise his sin. The satyrs were evil spirits. 12:3, *Libyans, Sukiim* and *Ethiopians* were troops from North Africa and the Sudan.

THOUGHT: The rapid decline in material standards was a result of spiritual laxity and disobedience; there was not an equally rapid return to wealth after the nation's repentance. Can any link be made nowadays between these two aspects of life?

13 Judah versus Israel

Abijah's short reign attracted the chronicler's interest it seems, for its illustration of God's continuing care for David's family. War between the northern tribes and the southern had been flickering throughout his father's reign (12:15), now Abijah evidently wanted to settle the matter. His army, and that of Jeroboam, was little smaller than David's at the time of the census (2 Sam. 24:9; 1 Chron. 21:5), although these numbers and that in v. 17 may not be literal (see Chronicles: *Introduction*). Abijah's troops advanced to the frontier point of Zemaraim (see Josh. 18:22) and it was there the king addressed his enemies, an ancient custom.

His words may have a self-righteous tone and elements of exaggeration, but they were aimed at demoralising the other side. With the breach between the tribes so recent that some would remember the old unity, it was suitable to speak in this way and to emphasise what should be done to honour God. The new worship was a human invention, no better than any other religion. God may only be approached and worshipped in the way he has commanded. The Lord who was 'God of Israel' was not the God which the northern tribes pretended lived at Bethel and Dan. Only Judah represented him, with his king at her head. But fine sentiments, however right, do not win battles! Israel's king had shown his skill in rising to the throne, now he showed it again. When Judah was all but lost, they cried to the Lord whom they claimed to be their God alone. If their faith was superficial before, it was real now (14,18). Israel was defeated, and Abijah moved his frontier forward a little.

1 Kings 15:3,4 tells that Abijah was not all his speech made out and that his preservation was for David's sake. Nor did the chronicler commend Abijah as he did his son (14:2).

Note: *a covenant of salt* (5): the preserving properties of salt made it suitable for figurative use in indicating a long-lasting quality.

THOUGHT: Abijah believed he was doing right even though he was not as orthodox as he claimed. His victory was not given as a reward or vindication. It is easy to assume that success means one is right. What premium should be set on orthodoxy?

Questions for further study and discussion on 2 Chronicles 1–13

1. Without the structure of a vital national religion with a visible shrine as its focal point, how may the church display the holiness and glory of God?

2. Solomon's wisdom is exemplified in the book of Proverbs; many chapters are addressed to 'my son', yet Solomon's real son apparently ignored his father's teaching. What does this tell us about the origin of the will to learn and do good?

3. Is Solomon's prayer in ch. 6 a form of bargain with God? What is its real basis and what is the Christian attitude to be (compare John 14,15)?

4. Consider the question of rewards and punishments (6:23,29,30). What does the New Testament add to these concepts?

5. Should Christians insist on an exclusive position, as Abijah did in ch. 13, when facing other religions? In what terms should a stand be stated?

14:1–15:15 A good king

Asa had the benefit of the victory God had given his father over Israel as his reign began. With the rest and peace he could give his attention to religious affairs without fear of his neighbour. Asa really practised what his father professed. The centres of pagan worship were abolished, whether public or private. At the same time, the kingdom's security was improved. Even so, the threat Zerah posed was as overwhelming as the one Abijah had faced and Asa, too, had to rely wholly on God. His prayer displays a faith absent from his father's speech (13:4–12). Its answer came in the total defeat of the enemy. The text makes it clear that this was not Asa's work: 'the Lord defeated the Ethiopians before Asa and before Judah . . . they were broken before the Lord and his army' (14:12,13). More than human forces were at war (compare Josh. 5:13,14). It was God's people who benefitted because of his action for them (14:14,15).

15:1–15 is one of the chronicler's contributions from a source not used in 1 Kings. It illustrates very well his concern for complete conformity to God's laws in religious observance as well as in daily life. Azariah's prophecy probably came after Asa's reforms and the victory over Zerah, for many saw that 'the Lord his God was with him' (15:9), although it could be understood as their cause. The task of abolishing all pagan worship in a society with poor communications and no police force cannot have been done swiftly, nor universally except over some time. An idol is more easily hidden than an altar. Azariah's words looked back to the days of the judges (15:5 see Judg. 5:6) The plain reciprocal relationship spoken of in 15:2 was recognised in the covenant the people subsequently made, which aimed at making the nation exclusive again. The people's purpose was sincere, bringing them joy and rest and knowledge of the Lord's presence. The oracle's words in 15:2 indicate that God is always ready to respond when his people truly seek him.

Note: *Zerah*, unknown from other records, may have been a general acting under orders from the pharaoh, son of Shishak (compare 12:9). *A million* (14:9) probably means 'innumerable'.

THOUGHT: 'Those who trust him wholly find him wholly true.' What idols are you tempted to hang on to?

15:16–16:14 Asa's decline

Asa's reforms were not simply imposed on his people, they willingly co-operated and the king made sure his own house was in order. Maacah was probably his grandmother (compare 11:20–22) and held a position of high honour as the senior surviving queen. While honour was due to her as a parent, her idolatry lost her any other. It was probably impossible to destroy the high places completely as many were simply hill tops, but artificial ones were demolished. Though it was not strictly correct to do so, some of the people may have been worshipping the Lord at the high places, so continued this practice despite Asa's reforms.

After a long and prosperous reign, Asa faced a new threat. He thought he could deal with it by diplomacy and succeeded in buying the Syrian king's help, turning him against Israel. Syrian forces invaded and conquered part of the Promised Land and its inhabitants. Judah was safe.

Asa secured his realm, but his method was wrong. Hanani soon showed him, but he did not want to hear. Clever he may have been, but he had initiated a type of policy that would bear bad fruit. He had involved an alien power in a dispute between the two parts of God's people. Asa needed help from a stronger power and should have turned to the God whose power he had experienced. Had he done so, he would have enjoyed unexpected success over the very Syrians he had hired (7,8)! As he did not seek God's help, the peace he sought would elude him. He even suffered physically because of his self-reliance; whether his doctors were competent or not, the king's complaint had a cause with which they were unable to cope.

Asa died and was buried with honour, for his reign had been marked by real religious reform, however much of his early faith had been lost.

Note: The *very great fire* (16:14) was apparently a mark of respect, not a cremation, which was very uncommon in the Old Testament period.

THOUGHT: Is there ever justification for involving secular authorities in disputes between Christians (compare 1 Cor. 6:1–8)? How do you act if a Christian quarrels with you? Remember Matthew 5:21–26.

17 Matters of authority

While it may not always be true that the good prosper, in Jehoshaphat's case it was so. However, he was not merely good in a passive way (6); *his heart was courageous* reveals a stance taken deliberately and a readiness to act. 17:1–16 summarises Jehoshaphat's reign: he secured his kingdom as best he could, he maintained the orthodoxy which his father had at first, and he fostered his people's faith. The result was God's blessing, seen in the prestige the king gained at home and abroad. The following verses expand on these events.

In the matter of faith (7–9) Jehoshaphat was not convinced that the people would follow his example. After sufficient time to establish himself and to discover the right men, he sent teachers to make sure everyone understood the faith. The teachers, men of standing and experience, represented both the social and administrative areas of life, and the sacred. The partnership of princes, Levites and priests reflects the all-pervading force of the law. The need for holiness in every part of the life of the individual and the community comes to the fore again. Holiness that was practised wholeheartedly would bring signs of God's favour. Notice that these leaders did not teach on their own authority, they had *the book of the law of the Lord with them* (9). Whatever they said was subject to the law and could be checked by it.

In politics (10–19) Jehoshaphat found his conduct at home brought recognition from his neighbours. Probably, like the chronicler, he would have attributed this to God's power (10), a fact acknowledged by foreigners too. They did not just observe God's intervention; they respected him and some (ch. 20) accepted his superiority. Their tribute contributed to Jehoshaphat's strength, and his own forces grew as the people were united by their common obedience to God's law.

Note: *the book of the law* may have been the five books of Moses, or parts of them. Theoretically, the priests and Levites scattered amongst the tribes in their various cities should have made sure that the people knew God's law. Through the centuries the system had broken down, especially with the division of Israel from Judah.

THOUGHT: The teaching Jehoshaphat instituted was done by taking God's law to the people where they were. What can your church learn from this and from the way it was done?

18:1–19:3 A question of authority

The compiler of 1 Kings gave Jehoshaphat little more attention than this episode. Here, in the context of the chronicler's longer account, the king of Judah's role is seen more clearly.

Solomon's glory had brought respect from foreigners, like the Queen of Sheba, and led him into perilous alliances by marriage; now Jehoshaphat took the same path. Alliance with Israel was better than war, so the marriage would appear to be sensible, yet it was condemned by God's spokesman (19:2) together with all that followed. Through the alliance, the king was drawn into an unnecessary war designed to glorify his apostate neighbour. Initially he was reluctant, he could not embark on such an action without clear approval from God. He was king but he was under the authority of God's word. After his rejection of Ahab's 'yes-men', it is surprising that Jehoshaphat did join Ahab's battle-march, for Micaiah's words were plain. Was Ahab so much stronger, or was Jehoshaphat unwilling to identify himself with the imprisoned prophet? He recognised Micaiah's authority, yet refused to follow his words or protect him. Stranger still is Jehoshaphat's ready connivance in Ahab's disguise, which does suggest he was very much the junior partner. He could hardly have been blind to the risk he ran! So Jehoshaphat was in the wrong place, allied with Ahab; fighting the wrong battle, disobedient to God's word. He suffered; yet God does not forsake his servants when, momentarily, they turn from him. *The Lord helped him* (18:31b) and he returned safely (19:1). Jehu the seer's blunt verdict drove the lesson home.

This episode raises inescapably the question of authority. Ahab bowed to no-one, he did what he wanted. Jehoshaphat knew that success lay in obedience to God's word. How could he know which advice was right when he heard it? Does 18:27 give the only answer (compare Deut. 13:1–11)? Could he expect God to guide him when he had allied himself to a wicked king? (The nature of Ahab's prophets is reflected in Ezek. 13.)

THOUGHT: How can I distinguish God's voice today from the many others advising me on what to do? Hebrews 1:2 tells of the highest authority; how much attention do I pay to his words and to the teaching of his appointed spokesmen in the New Testament?

19:4–20:37 Jehoshaphat's justices and God's justice

Chastened, Jehoshaphat turned to the further reform of society in Judah. He himself toured his realm, inspecting its affairs as a good shepherd, even a moment's inattention could see a decline in faith. Evidently justice had not been administered equitably, the abuses Amos condemned (eg. Amos 5:7,12) had appeared. Justice is, by definition, impartial. When God's laws are administered in his name, it has to be utterly beyond suspicion. The judges were to share the same 'fear' of God (19:7) as Jehoshaphat's neighbours (17:10), aware that he is the living God. In the capital was a special panel, a court of appeal, constituted so as to represent all interests, civil and religious, and to look at all sides of a case. Its members were still under the authority of the law, and were to apply it fearlessly (19:11). Overall responsibility for justice in the land was vested in the high priest and the king's minister, whose attention was directed, we may assume, to such matters as taxation, military service and royal commands. The high priest's involvement in justice was of extraordinary importance in the light of his role as the people's representative in the annual atonement ceremony when he offered a sacrifice in respect of the nation's sins and re-established their holiness.

Judah's eastern neighbours attacked, perhaps after the inconclusive campaign reported in 2 Kings 3. Jehoshaphat's reactions may be compared with Hezekiah's (ch. 32). He called for God to act in order that his plan in creating his people might not be frustrated. Since Israel did not harm the enemy when she had the opportunity, the enemy was wrong to attack. As God had fought for Asa, so he did now for Jehoshaphat. Those who object to the idea of God intervening in history explain the enemy's demise in terms of the poor liaison within their coalition. But the writer's concern here is to specify the cause of their defeat, not details of the means. So God acted justly and his people benefitted.

The account of the Tarshish ships incident, different from 1 Kings 22:48,49 probably through compression, explores the course of another alliance with his faithless neighbour that ended in disaster for Jehoshaphat.

Note: *the Meunites* (20:1) were a little-known tribe south of Judah.

THOUGHT: Was the attack on Judah a fulfilment of the verdict in 19:2? Can a Christian expect to go through life without attacks? Why does God allow them?

21 A base king

Jehoshaphat tried to treat his sons fairly so that they would not envy their elder brother his throne. Yet Jehoshaphat's own policies had sown the seeds of the bloodshed that followed his death, for his ill-advised alliance with Ahab had resulted in his heir marrying Ahab's daughter, Athaliah. Verse 6 shows plainly how that affected the new king; whatever the strength of his father's good example, his wife and her family had greater influence. We may speculate that Jehoram's brothers opposed his attitude out of loyalty to their father's faith; there is no suggestion that they were threatening his. Contrast Jehoram's treatment of his brothers with God's treatment of him. The man could not keep faith with his own generation, whereas God was faithful to six.

Despite Jehoram's success against Edomite forces, his army fled (see 2 Kings 8:21). He failed to maintain the repute his father had gained among his neighbours as a direct result of his apostasy. Enemy attacks reduced the realm, its wealth, and its prestige. King and people suffered. All Jehoshaphat's faithfulness in loyalty to God seemed to be cancelled out by the paganism which was re-instated. Jehoram's actions were a calculated rejection of the high standards God demanded. Elijah's letter is as forthright as he ever was with Ahab; the RSV translation, *led into unfaithfulness*, lacks the force of the Hebrew, *led to prostitute themselves* (see AV, RV, NIV). 2 Kings 3:11 suggests Elijah had died earlier; if so, he may have left a prepared letter, foreseeing the road Jehoram would take, but the text need not be so read.

God's control of the nations is well displayed in the contrast of 17:10 with 21:16. Jehoram forfeited the privilege of family life (17), then of royal respect (19), retaining only the worst of epitaphs (20).

Notes: The second *Azariah* in v. 2 may be a simple error for Uzziah, only one letter different in Hebrew. *The Arabs near the Ethiopians* (16) lived on the borders of Egypt, which was ruled at that time by a dynasty from the Sudan, compare 14:9ff.

THOUGHT: You cannot serve two masters. Elijah's message put this as starkly as the Lord did (Matt. 6:19–24). Have I taken the warning to heart? Whose suggestions do I follow?

22;23 The evil interlude reversed

Despite Jehoram's unpopularity and the destruction of almost all his family, David's line still commanded the people's loyalty, so they made Jehoram's sole surviving son king. The baleful influence of the alliance with Ahab continued through Jehoash's short reign. His friendly act toward Jehoram of Israel led to his death; see 2 Kings 9. The chronicler gives a summary (22:8,9) which should not be seen as a list of events in exact order, contrary to the Kings account.

Ahaziah's death *was ordained by God* (22:7) yet it allowed the queen mother, Athaliah, free reign. For six years she was able to encourage the paganism of her family in Judah. She had lost all her own sons but went on to slaughter her grandsons, thereby apparently spoiling the succession. Was she planning to join Judah to Israel, or to set up a new dynasty? As Elijah had learned, God knows those who are faithful to him, even when evil appears triumphant. The satanic queen was frustrated by the loyal princess, the priest's wife, so a scion of David was saved.

Jehoiada's rebellion and Athaliah's death are related almost identically in 2 Kings 11. The priest took care that everything should be done efficiently, and the chronicler noted the role of the Levites. The priest's aim was clear: to bring Judah back to God. Failure would have brought disaster. Any activity done on God's behalf, even a *coup d'état*, demands the highest standards in accord with his holiness. Only when the movement was well under way did Athaliah realise what was afoot. For *her* to cry 'Treason' was ironic, yet those who do evil, like her, so often assert their integrity and claim the rights they deny to others.

Note: *forty-two years* (22:2) would make him two years older than his father (see 21:20)! 2 Kings 8:26 has twenty-two, indicating a scribal error here. *Samaria* (22:9) – 2 Kings 9:27 has a different location, so this name may cover an adjacent region.

THOUGHT: How particular should a Christian be about purity in God's service (see 23:19)?

Questions for further study and discussion on 2 Chronicles 14–23

1. Do you see any danger of a parallel between Asa's career (14–16) and the pattern of your own Christian life?

2. Note 16:9a, compared with Zechariah 4:10. At one time the king's secret agents were called his 'eyes and ears', but God's purpose is to bless. He is always faithful but his servants have to maintain their attitude. How is this both a comfort and a challenge?

3. Jehoshaphat's alliance with Ahab can be seen as a result of pride: a powerful potential enemy was willing to be his friend. Trace the stages of Jehoshaphat's increasing entanglement and how God's grace alone saved him. Success and honour in a career can quickly lead us into a similar situation. Examine your present commitments in the light of 19:2.

4. Compare the conduct of Jehoshaphat's army (20:20–22) with the conduct of Paul and Silas (Acts 16:22–34). How do you react in adversity and what impression does your conduct make on others?

5. True and false prophets (ch. 18) were at work in the early church (eg. Acts 13:6; 1 John 4). With the canon of scripture complete, the function of a prophet today may be different. Study 1 Corinthians 14 with particular attention to the cautions in verses 3,24,29–33,37–40.

24 Joash: from good to bad

Joash began to reign under the tutelage of Jehoiada, but not under his thumb, as v. 6 reveals! Restoring God's temple was an act of piety, it was also the duty of any self-respecting king as it showed his wealth and standing. Joash's impatience can be understood in this light, delay reflected badly on him. Royal resources and the temple funds were inadequate for making good the neglected building and its equipment. Public contributions were solicited, the collection box being set up at the entry where an altar stood (8, see also 2 Kings 12:9), a reminder that the offering was to be as much for God as for the king's prestige. Enough entered the chest to complete the work on the building and to provide all that was needed for the services, such was the response of God's people. Yet all rested on the inspiration of Jehoiada, and with his death Joash lost his mentor.

Despite the good Jehoiada had done, he had no successor of the same calibre and Joash lacked the stability to sustain the reformed faith. His new advisors soon led him to the old, easy ways of his father and grandfather. Perhaps it was in the hope of stifling a guilty conscience that Joash committed his crime against Jehoiada's son, silencing the prophet's unwelcome rebukes. Zechariah's death was not an act of violence, done on the spur of the moment, but something plotted, like Naboth's (1 Kings 21:10), possibly with a similar charge. The stoning within the temple precinct was another sign of Joash's revolt against God's law (compare 23:14). Zechariah's death, falling towards the end of 2 Chronicles, the last book of the Hebrew Old Testament, made a convenient point of reference for Jesus when he condemned the Jews as a whole for their wilful disregard of God's spokesmen (Matt. 23:35; Luke 11:51. Note that 'son of Berechiah' of Matt. 23 may be a mistaken addition; it is absent from Luke 11 and the oldest surviving copy of Matt.).

The only language Israel seemed to understand when she rejected God was the language of military defeat. The Syrians had a case against Judah because she had helped Israel against her, and Judah crumbled. Happily for Judah, not all had forsaken the orthodox way; but notice that one had an Ammonite for his mother, and the other a Moabite. God's people never had an exclusively nationalist basis; God's Israel embraced all who accepted his Law, compare Galatians 3:28.

THOUGHT: No explanation is given for Joash's change of faith, but he is shown to be first under Jehoiada's guidance, and then under the guidance of others. What does this teach us about the relative importance of guides and personal conviction?

25; 26 A failure of faith and a failure of conduct

Amaziah. Much of chapter 25 repeats 2 Kings 14, but verses 5–16 relate in detail the campaign covered in one verse there. The verdict on Amaziah is good overall, but not unreservedly so (25:2). Amaziah began by executing his father's assassins, the due punishment even though concern for justice had motivated their action (24:25), for no society can permit individuals to take the law into their own hands. The census (25:5) showed that Judah's military strength had decreased by two-thirds since the days of Jehoshaphat (17:14–18), so the king hired soldiers from the north at three shekels a head, no small sum – a slave cost about fifty shekels (see on 2 Kings 15:20). On the prophet's advice, these hired men from apostate Israel were dismissed. Amaziah was worried about his financial loss and his country paid more as the men returned home. Real faith from the first would have cost Amaziah and his people less. The prophet's words (25:7,8) are obscure, as comparison of the RV, RSV, and NIV will show. They may be a warning that God would not favour Amaziah if he kept his mercenaries, or, by a slight alteration of the Hebrew, they may be an encouragement to fight, assuming the Israelites were sent away. The attack was successful, but Amaziah apparently thought Edom's gods were helping him, and wanted to retain their goodwill. Failure to obey the prophet's words was followed by a final display of pride, bringing disaster and a death like his father's.

Uzziah. Uzziah's reign is reported with more detail here than in 2 Kings 14,15. It was a period of recovery. Troublesome neighbours (Philistines, Arabs, Meunites, see 17:11; 21:16) were subdued and the kingdom was strengthened. Successful in his kingly role, Uzziah felt impelled to act the priest as well. Those who tried to stop him were not merely sustaining a 'closed shop', they were preserving God's order which laid a premium on his holiness. (Korah and his company had died for a comparable offence, Num. 16; note v. 40.) Uzziah lived the rest of his life as an illustration of the reality of holiness. He could never enter God's temple again.

THOUGHT: Amaziah seems really to have had more faith in himself than in God. Uzziah thought he was great enough to break God's ritual rules. How often do I fall to such temptations? See Matthew 18:1–4.

27; 28 The feebly good and the actively bad

Jotham's reign saw continuing prosperity, strengthening of the realm and further tribute from Ammon across the Jordan. The *forts and towers* apparently formed a chain to guard against raiders and give warning of their approach. Jotham was faithful to God himself (27:6) but there is no hint that he tried to guide his people; they followed their own easy way, paying lip-service to the Lord, while worshipping the idols which made no heavy demands on their conduct (27:2).

Ahaz, Jotham's son, was determinedly perverse. The account in Chronicles introduces an incident absent from 2 Kings 16 and presents others in a different light. Politically, Ahaz seemed to be at the mercy of his stronger neighbours in Samaria and Damascus, allied, it appears, against a threat from Assyria. The only hope that Ahaz could see lay in securing Assyria's friendship and aid. The warnings of the prophet Isaiah (Isa. ch. 7) went unheeded. Yet the relief Ahaz obtained was small. Damascus and Samaria were taken by the Assyrians, so no longer loomed over Judah, but Ahaz became a vassal to Assyria, Judah a client kingdom, and had to pay an annual tribute. There was a loss of much territory to the south and west, too. Religiously, Ahaz was rootless. He worshipped pagan gods and offered his children in a way absolutely forbidden to God's people (Deut. 18:10) but well-attested in the Phoenician city of Carthage where large numbers of infant cremations have been found. When such acts failed to bring him success, he turned to other gods from abroad, then closed the temple proper to orthodox worship. His only fixed idea, we may deduce, was to deny the true God.

Yet even in Israel God still had his spokesman. As the victorious troops herded their Judean captives towards Samaria, they were met by leaders whose authority they evidently accepted and who respected Oded's words. The prisoners were sent home with adequate provisions. Wholesale deportations were practised by the major powers and Israel was to suffer in this way soon afterwards, but for one small nation to treat another in this way was felt to be a great crime (compare Amos 1:6,9).

Note: The events of 28:22–25 probably refer to the defeat described in 28:5 when Syria appeared to be supreme, rather than to Ahaz's visit to Damascus when Assyria had taken it (2 Kings 16:10).

THOUGHT: 'Actions speak louder than words'. A Christian's example may have some effect, but its influence will not last long without an explanation and an invitation to others to follow it.

29 Hezekiah's reform: (1) repentance

Despite all the evil of wicked men, God's truth remains known; someone had taught Ahaz's son God's way and he had accepted it. No sooner was he on the throne than he acted (3). This time the whole system of worship had to be cleansed – holy place, priests, Levites and nation. God's own temple was unfit for his worship so long as heathen objects were there; his priests could not function because the sacrifices had ceased which assured their purity, and the people could not worship because no atonement had been offered for their sins. The covenant was forgotten. Once the place was prepared, the people could come to God. Once sin offerings and burnt offerings had been made, everyone could praise God, for the burning symbolised his acceptance. Thereafter individuals could bring their own sacrifices, including the 'peace offering' (35) of which they ate part.

The sin offering was made first because, through it, pardon was found for offences against God. The burnt offering could have the same value, but is best seen as an outright gift to God as a worshipper recognised his Person. The other offerings were shared with the temple staff. Notice the identification of the penitent king and people with the sin-offering (23), and the significant role of the blood. Here is a clear illustration of the value of sacrifice as a substitution for the sacrificer. Judah had been rendered all but powerless: she had drawn Assyrian forces into the area and was, no doubt, despised by other nations for doing so. Judah's lack of trust had also angered God and he was on his way to destroy her in his anger (8–10).

As people and king repented, their sacrifices were accepted in place of further suffering. Thus they could rejoice. After barely a fortnight the proper order was restored. There were no lengthy, arduous preparations that might have had a discouraging effect; the time was ripe, and God's man was ready (36). The chronicler notes that it was all God's doing, not simply the will or the whim of king or people. Nevertheless, it resounds to the credit of Hezekiah, new to the throne, that this was his prime task. His father was dead, yet he had to make the sacrifices to rectify what his father had put wrong, and he had to lead the people.

THOUGHT: Compare Hezekiah's position with your own; see Romans 5:6–11.

30; 31 Hezekiah's reform: (2) passover and offerings

Once the people had re-established their communion with God it was important that they began to follow the religious calendar again. A few had evidently kept the passover through the years of Ahaz's apostasy (30:5) but the significance of the festival was primarily national, it recalled the foundation of Israel. Each family was required to observe it, emphasising that the nation consisted of individual families, but when only a few remembered it the impact was lost. Israel owed her existence to God's grace and power in bringing her out of Egypt, and to nothing else. Regular remembrance of that fact by all the people was a powerful aid to faith in times of hardship and of prosperity. The king now tried to bring all Israel together, for the division of the north from Judah was political, not religious, in origin, even though those who lived in the north were part of an Assyrian province.

The unusual circumstances brought the passover into the second month rather than the first (30:2,3), a possibility envisaged in Numbers 9:6–13. Even then, there were some who did not meet the qualifications of ritual purity. For them there was no possibility of waiting until the next month, for the sense of solidarity in the national festival would be too greatly diluted if it were celebrated so long after the true anniversary. Yet they were citizens of the northern region, the ones whom Hezekiah had tried so particularly to embrace; they could hardly be sent home and told to wait until next year. Hezekiah's vision was wide enough to take them into the festival and deep enough to see that their hearts' condition mattered more than their physical state.

Hezekiah's devotion and generous care for his people (30:18,19,22,24; 31:3) elicited parallel generosity from them. First-fruits and tithes were prescribed to maintain the priests (Num. 18:12,13) and the Levites (Num. 18:20–24) so that they could be free from concern about providing for their families when they were serving in the temple; on this occasion more than enough was given through the people's faithfulness to their obligations (31:12). Now so much was available, arrangements had to be made for an equitable distribution to all who were eligible to receive the gifts (31:12–19; compare Acts 6:1).

THOUGHT: The tithes and first-fruits were regular, expected offerings. When everyone played his part there was more than sufficient. Does your church suffer, or some other part of the work of God, because your giving falls short of this standard?

32 Hezekiah faces trials

For the chronicler Hezekiah's religious reforms were most important, perhaps the more so as they receive minimal mention in 2 Kings 18:3–6. However, they did not eclipse the momentous political history. Judah's parlous state is made plain, the Assyrians attacked all Hezekiah's towns and laid seige to Jerusalem. The king had prepared his capital to resist, but he knew that his defensive works alone were inadequate (8). Eventually his faith was vindicated (23).

How would he have viewed the Assyrian onslaught? One aim of his reforms was to avert the wrath of the Lord (29:10) and the chronicler himself may admit a little surprise at the turn of events by his opening words, *these acts of faithfulness*. Politically, Hezekiah was in the wrong as a rebellious vassal, breaking the oaths his father had sworn to obtain Assyrian help. The invasion, therefore, was a consequence of *Ahaz's* reliance on human arms rather than God. To the people of the towns and countryside it would appear as punishment for their earlier idolatry. Yet had they not been punished already (29:8,9)? By summarising the Assyrian propaganda (10–15,17) which 2 Kings reports at length, the chronicler surely intended to explain that Sennacherib's campaign was a test for Hezekiah and his subjects, and a means of demonstrating the power of God. Whatever arguments may be advanced on more or less rationalistic grounds to account for the angel of v. 21, it is a fact that Sennacherib failed to capture Jerusalem and was later murdered by some of his sons.

Having passed the great public test, Hezekiah was faced with a more personal one, and failed (24–26). He soon saw his error and sought forgiveness. Nevertheless, the consequences could not be cancelled; if he did not suffer them all, his people did.

Pride caught him, too, when the impressive embassy arrived from far-off Babylon. They came because of the 'sign' (2 Kings 20:12). The king again regarded as his own what should have been for God's glory (2 Kings 20:13–15). All he had came from God (23,27–29).

Note: With reference to verses 4 and 30, a Hebrew inscription found in the tunnel running underneath the city, from the spring of Gihon (the Virgin's Fountain) to the Pool of Siloam, is thought to date from the works of Hezekiah.

THOUGHT: 'Therefore wrath came upon him' (25). Do we recognise God's anger, how we bring it upon ourselves, and how that can affect others? Can Hezekiah's example teach us how to avoid it?

33 A great sinner converted

The centralised, regulated orthodoxy of Hezekiah offered little scope to his son's young mind. Bereft of his father just as he began to grow up, Manasseh did not, apparently, have any wise counsellor whom he could trust. He turned from the narrow paths of righteousness to the libertarianism of the ancient pagan fertility cults. With youthful zeal he fostered their rites and set up their furniture throughout his kingdom, especially in the capital. There the true Owner was displaced from his temple and his name was scorned. His command that no images be made was brazenly flouted. How Manasseh treated those who were quietly faithful to his father's ways we are not told (but see comment on 2 Kings 21). If he persecuted some, he simply threw into relief the mercy God displayed in continuing to speak to his people, offering the choice of repentance (12,13).

The fate Hezekiah escaped, because of his faith, befell his son. Manasseh was taken prisoner by the Assyrians and carried away to their land. Their inscriptions name him, but not as a captive. There is no need to doubt the truth of the story as many commentators do. It can be placed towards the end of Manasseh's reign, about 650 bc, at a time of widespread anti-Assyrian plotting. The fact that Manasseh was taken to Babylon gives credence to this for the Assyrian king conquered the city and set about repairing and restoring its temples. That Manasseh should turn about politically and religiously, is also conceivable and acceptable. There is no need to suppose that his repentance was a fiction to remove the difficulty which a long reign of wickedness may be thought to pose to a simplistic theology of 'good=prosperity; evil=disgrace and death'. Other subject kings were deported to Assyria for mutiny, then repatriated under new oaths of loyalty. Other men, too, have repented after years spent defying God and his laws. Regrettably, a late repentance cannot obliterate the effects of the earlier evil. Manasseh's own *volte-face* could not cancel all his previous encouragement of heathenism, so truly correct worship was not restored (17). Most notably, Amon, his son, had passed his formative years under Manasseh's tutelage in evil. His two years' reign was so bad that his own courtiers killed him. Even so, they had to be punished, and the popular loyalty to David's family was demonstrated by continuing the succession through his son.

THOUGHT: Hezekiah's pride (32:24–26) and Manasseh's sin brought trouble for many people. How often do our failures do that? How much of ourselves and of our possessions do we offer to God in gratitude for the grace brought by 'that One Man' of Romans 5:15?

34; 35 Good king Josiah

Manasseh's grandson, Josiah, made a conscious decision to reverse his father's policy when he was fifteen or sixteen years old. After four years he was sure enough of his faith and its meaning to act firmly. His grandfather had made some amends (33:15,16); Josiah ensured the end of overt heathenism as long as he was on the throne. Destroying the idols and altars was decisive, but he went further and desecrated them so that they could not be used surreptitiously (34:4,5,7). Josiah knew what Jesus later taught so vividly in the parable in Luke 11:24–26. He went on to restore the temple (compare 2 Kings 22). Typically, the chronicler gave the names of the officers responsible for the work and noted the role of the Levites in providing music to keep the labourers working in rhythm.

Josiah's faith may have rested on the records of his good ancestors and the teachings of the prophets; Micah and Isaiah preached a little before his time, Nahum and Zephaniah were active early in his reign. Clearly he was unaware of the details of the law until the book was found so unexpectedly. Papyrus or leather scrolls could survive for centuries in a dry place and this one may have been very old. However old, its words spoke plainly to the king and he knew the words spelt danger. Anyone who reads Deuteronomy will see why, especially from ch. 27 onwards.

As Hezekiah had done, Josiah called the people to remember their insignificant origins and the great, unmerited work God had done for them. He celebrated the passover with more care than had been seen for centuries. With the lambs there were other animals, all prepared in the proper way – the lambs roasted, the oxen and others boiled (see 1 Sam. 2:14). The dates (35:1,19) may indicate that the passover was kept before the law-book was found (34:8), or immediately after as a result of the find.

Josiah was less careful in his diplomacy. Did he see a threat in the growing power of Egypt? Necho assured him there was none. Was he seeking a triumph to add fame to his name? Josiah's death came through his stupidity; he fought an unnecessary battle, and lost.

Note: The Levites (35:3) in an excess of zeal seem to have reverted to an activity prescribed for the wilderness era (Num. 4) as if the whole of the exodus was to be re-enacted.

THOUGHT: Was Josiah so immersed in the book of the law that he could not recognise God's word spoken by a foreign king (35:22)? How may we learn to identify God's voice outside the Bible?

36 Judah's death and re-birth

After Josiah's rash interference, Judah rapidly declined, subjugated first by Egypt, then by Babylon. 2 Kings 23,24 and Jeremiah 39–44,52 tell the sad details. Here the chronicler ends his work with an outline. He points to the reasons for the fall of Jerusalem (14–16). Kings, priests and people were each as bad as the other. King Zedekiah was not even faithful to his imperial master (13). The capital's fate was extreme, slaughter or exile for citizens, looting and destruction for the buildings. The punishment was sent both by Nebuchadnezzar, for Zedekiah's infidelity after Jehoiakim's, and also by God, for Judah's religious faithlessness. Even the symbols of God's presence were removed; his promises (as in 33:4) were not designed to permit his people unlimited apostasy, there came an end to his day of grace.

The Promised Land was left almost empty, it was not repopulated with aliens as Samaria had been (2 Kings 17:24). Thus it could rest and make up for the sabbaths, the fallow years which should have been kept every seventh year (Lev. 25:1–7). Throughout the history of Israel the land was integral to the nation and even in moments of destruction Jeremiah looked for restoration. So the chronicler could not end on an entirely black note. His closing verses overlap with Ezra 1, showing the continuity of the history of God's people, reminding those of his own day that they were descendants of those whose often disgraceful conduct he had related. His use of Cyrus' words to close the book served as a further reminder that Israel's God was not restricted to using only Israelites to further his purposes. Notice that Cyrus' 'decree' exhorts rather than commands the exiled Jews, and so reflects God's attitude which does not compel, but invites, men to come to him. Their acceptance brings them responsibilities towards him, and the chronicler's books show those to us: 'If you love me, keep my commands'. The commencement of Chronicles with Adam and their completion with the return from exile also illustrates a common biblical theme: the good start, followed by a decline, then the promise or prospect of a return to the first position, or a better one. This is also a major theme of the New Testament and so unites both parts of the Bible.

Note: Ezra and Nehemiah stand before Chronicles in the Hebrew Bible, so 36:22,23 are more important as a link to them there than in English versions.

THOUGHT: Despite his predominantly gloomy story, the chronicler records with care the names of faithful men who ensured that God's word and will were not forgotten. How can you help your church to survive as a bastion of God's truth?

Questions for further study and discussion on 2 Chronicles 24–36

1. Tyrannicides, like Zabad and Jehozabad (24:26), may be hailed as heroes in modern society. Should they receive any reward other than that stated in 25:3 (compare Matt. 26:52)?

2. Zechariah, dying, called for vengeance (24:22). Stephen, dying, called for God to pardon his executioners (Acts 7:60). Are these thoughts irreconcilable? Deuteronomy 32 illustrates God's avenging activity well. Study other passages on this topic with the aid of a concordance. Should a Christian ever seek to avenge his brother's hurt?

3. Jotham seems to have followed a *laissez faire* policy; he 'walked steadfastly before the Lord' (27:6, NIV) while leaving his people to do as they pleased, which was to ignore God's ways. How far did this contribute to the success of Ahaz's paganising policy? How can we follow the exhortations of Galatians 6:1–5 and 1 John 5:16 today? Is it, in fact, better to leave others to do as they please, Christian or not?

4. Hezekiah's vigorous action (29) after Ahaz's evil reign soon restored the supremacy of truth, yet only for as long as he reigned (see ch. 33). How can churches guard against such violent changes?

5. Does 30:18–20 imply anything for church discipline? If so, what, and why?